GROWING FRUIT

GROWING FRUIT

Alan Mansfield

THE CROWOOD PRESS

First published in 2012 by
The Crowood Press Ltd
Ramsbury, Marlborough
Wiltshire SN8 2HR

www.crowood.com

© Alan Mansfield 2012

British Library Cataloguing-in-Publication Data
A catalogue record for this book is available from the British Library.

ISBN 978 1 84797 389 4

Dedication
Thanks to Sal, who managed to get me organized to complete this book, and to members of the RHS Fruit Group, a friendly bunch who have generously shared with me their knowledge of fruit and experience of fruit growing.

Typeset by Jean Cussons Typesetting, Diss, Norfolk
Printed and bound in Malaysia by Times Offset (M) Sdn Bhd

CONTENTS

INTRODUCTION

Gardeners often worry about growing fruit, seeing it as something that is complicated and best left to the experts, but don't worry – fruit has been grown successfully in this country since pre-Roman times. Over the centuries the varieties may have become more refined and developed, and we may now give names to the varieties, but the basic skills and techniques for growing fruit successfully have not really changed.

Left to grow undisturbed, fruit trees will do nothing but produce fruit for their own reproduction. Growing fruit is about managing the shape and size of the fruit tree to produce the best quality fruit in quantities that satisfy the grower and do not exhaust the tree.

Growing fruit is a lovely way to spend your time, and I wish all readers great success. And remember, if you do not manage to produce fruit this year, don't worry – there's always next year.

OPPOSITE: **Left to grow undisturbed, fruit trees will do nothing but produce fruit – like this Malus *Golden Hornet*.**

WHAT WOULD YOU LIKE TO GROW?

Decisions

In a perfect world, with unlimited space, time and resources, it would be lovely to grow trees of every type of fruit, a veritable Garden of Eden. But few of us have that luxury, and will be constrained by garden size, space available, growing conditions, money to spend on fruit trees and time available to cultivate all those trees. So decisions will have to be made.

Which Fruit?

The first and pretty fundamental decision is which fruit to grow? We each have favourite fruit, which is as good a starting point as any – grow the fruit you like. Think about which fruit you buy the most, which you use most for eating or cooking. Linked to this is the commercial reality that in the shops some fruit cost more than others to buy – if space is limited, it would make sense to grow the fruit that is the most expensive to buy. Why take up space growing something that sells relatively cheaply, such as *Bramley's Seedling* apples, when the same space could grow something that is more expensive, such as raspberries.

Soft Fruit

Soft fruit is the term used collectively for the currants and berried fruit that tends to ripen during the summer and early autumn. This includes redcurrants,

OPPOSITE PAGE: **Colourful flowers attract bees and other pollinating insects into the fruit garden.**

white currants and blackcurrants, cane fruit such as raspberries, loganberries and blackberries, the increasingly popular blueberry, and, of course, the strawberry. Together, soft fruits define 'summer' for the fruit grower. In general, soft fruits are relatively easy to grow; they take up little space, or can be grown to fit the space available; they look very attractive, growing in the garden, and are filled to bursting with vitamins and trace elements to help keep us healthy. One final point about soft fruit is that they tend to be the most expensive to buy from the supermarket, so a row of raspberries or blueberries will really help with the household budget and help provide the family with their 'five-a-day'.

White currants, pink currants and redcurrants: tasty soft fruit.

Tree Fruit

Tree fruit or top fruit are terms used to group together the different types of fruit that grow on trees, such as apple, apricot, cherry, peach, pear, plum, quince, etc. If you are planning to grow any of these, there are some general decisions that will need to be made, which will produce a shopping list to take to the nursery or garden centre. Fruit trees are quite expensive to buy, so mistakes can be costly. A little research and planning can help you find a fruit tree that is right for you and your garden.

Variety

Having selected which fruit to grow, the next decision is which variety? The National Fruit Collection at Brogdale in Kent grows around 2,000 apples, 500 pears, 300 plums, 280 cherries, 19 quinces, 50 hazelnuts, 150 gooseberries and 200 currants (black, red, white and pink), each being a different cultivar

GROWING FRUIT – BUYING CHECKLIST

Fruit trees, bushes and plants are often bought on impulse, which is fine, but before the decision is made a quick glance at this checklist will help to increase the chances of a good crop, and to avoid costly mistakes.

If you grow your own, you don't need to buy your five-a-day!

Which fruit? what do I like to eat, which do I want to grow? Is this appropriate for growing conditions?

Which varieties? which are my favourites for eating and cooking?

Pollination: will the chosen varieties (two or more) pollinate each other?

Location and space: where will the fruit be growing?

Form: how will the fruit be trained?

Rootstock: is this an issue? If so, which is best for the chosen location, space and training method?

Fruit trees in flower at the National Fruit Collection at Brogdale in Kent.

or variety. Plant Heritage run the National Collection Scheme, bringing together other fruit collections, each holding many different varieties. So how do you choose?

The most direct way is to taste the fruit and identify which ones you like best. Fruit tastings are often organized as part of fruit shows or at fruit-oriented events like the Apple Day celebrations that take place all over the country in the autumn. Another way is to buy and try different fruit being sold at farm shops and farmers' markets, which offer a wide range of varieties of seasonal fruit.

Another factor in choosing which varieties of fruit to grow relates to the climatic and cultivation conditions in your area. There are likely to be regional or even local types of fruit that have been grown historically in your area – if a particular variety has been grown there for many years, the chances are that it will be successful in your garden. Choosing varieties that grow well in your area will make a big difference to how successful you will be in your garden – it is often wiser to choose a variety that enjoys local conditions, rather than struggle to grow a variety that is not suitable. For example, apples that fare well in the milder, wetter conditions of the south-west of England, such as *Irish Peach* or *Cornish Gillyflower*, will not grow or fruit well in northern counties where the weather is harsher. Conversely, apples such as *Gala* that grow scab-free in cooler, dryer parts of the country will quickly succumb to the problem if grown in the wetter west of the country.

Of course, it makes sense to choose varieties that offer some resistance to the most common diseases; doing this will help keep your fruit trees healthy, reduce the amount of the crop lost to disease and generally make the fruit more attractive to eat. Also, disease-resistant varieties will reduce the angst and worry over dealing with problems related to the fruit, and remove or at least reduce the need to resort to chemicals to sort out health issues related to fruit trees.

Fashion also has a part to play, with different fruits falling in and out of favour over time. *Cox's Orange Pippin* is generally regarded as Britain's 'favourite apple' and indeed it does have a unique and splendid flavour, but it is not the easiest apple to grow, especially along organic principles, as it is very susceptible to powdery mildew. Similarly, the popularity of *Braeburn* apples in the supermarkets has meant that *Braeburn* trees are commonly available in garden centres, but again this is not the easiest apple to grow; raised in New Zealand, it requires a really good summer in the UK to ripen to the point where it develops the flavour of *Braeburns* grown in warmer climes. Conversely, the *Golden Delicious* apple, which has had a bad press as a result of being hard and tasteless when bought in a supermarket, will produce really tasty fruit if grown in British gardens and left to ripen fully on the tree

before being picked in the late autumn, when it has had a chance to ripen and mature in flavour.

In the world of soft fruit, the poor old gooseberry seems to have gone out of favour, pushed aside by the promotion of blueberries as a 'super fruit'. As a result, few retailers stock gooseberries, which means that fewer people have the chance to buy them; lower sales means that fewer people are cooking and eating them, which means that fewer people know what to do with them, so sales continue their downward spiral. Fruit growers can reverse this trend in their own gardens by growing gooseberries and showing family and friends just what a tasty and versatile fruit they can be.

Finally, your choice of varieties may be limited to what is available in local nurseries or garden centres, where the stock will have been chosen by someone who has made the basic decision for you. Good nurseries and garden centres are likely to stock varieties that suit local conditions and are unlikely to sell something that is really not suitable, as this could result in failure for the customer and consequent complaints and potential loss of business in the future. However, some outlets will sell anything that attracts the eye of the customer, whether it is suitable or not, relying on the fact that beginners to fruit growing are more likely to attribute failure to their own lack of experience, rather than blame the retailer for selling them an inappropriate plant. If in doubt, ask for advice.

Cox's Orange Pippin: **'Britain's Favourite Apple'.**

Pollination

Pollination plays a really important part in the selection of fruit trees, although this is not really an issue for soft fruit, most of which are self-fertile. One exception is the blueberry, which is self-fertile to some degree, but will produce a better crop of better quality fruit if a second blueberry of a different variety is grown nearby to cross-pollinate. In fact, most tree fruit will also be self-fertile to some extent, but the crop will be increased in size and quality if pollen from a second tree, a different variety of the same fruit, is available for effective cross-pollination.

This means that you may need to grow two fruit trees: two apples, two pears, etc., each being a different variety that will have its flowers open and producing pollen at the same time – unless, of course, there are other fruit trees in the neighbourhood which can provide pollen for your tree. Some fruit trees do not set viable pollen, which means that they will not pollinate a second tree; in this situation, a third tree must be grown for the effective pollination of all the fruit in the collection. Family trees overcome this problem by having two or three different varieties growing on a single tree.

Most fruit trees are pollinated by insects, so another factor in effective pollination is the weather. Too cold or too wet and the insects will not fly. Although the honeybee is popularly thought of as the insect that pollinates fruit, and in some areas at different times of the year it may well be the main pollinator, there are a number of other insects that will also do the job. These include bumblebees, solitary bees like the mason bee, hoverflies, flower and pollen beetles, butterflies and moths; even wasps and some species of fly will play their part in the pollination process.

If all else fails, or if you want to make sure that pollination occurs, you can always carry out the insects'

job yourself, with the aid of a soft, watercolour artist's paintbrush. This can be most effective for peaches, nectarines or apricots, which come into flower early in the spring when the weather may be too cold for pollinating insects to fly. Choose a warm sunny day when the flowers on the fruit tree are open fully and the pollen is 'ripe' – that is, when you can see dusty yellow pollen on the anthers of the flowers. Use the tip of the brush to transfer the pollen gently from the anthers to the stigma of the flower, which is usually located right in the centre of the flower, glistening and receptive to the pollen. To make sure that pollination is really effective, this operation may need to be done on a number of different days, as the flowers open and the pollen ripens.

Pollination Groups

To help fruit growers make sure that pollination will be effective, some types of fruit tree – apples, pears, plums and cherries – are listed in groups, based on when they come into flower. By selecting trees from the same flowering group you can ensure that the trees will flower at more or less the same time, mean-

Groups of apple trees in flower at the National Fruit Collection at Brogdale in Kent.

ing that there will be pollen available for each tree when required. In fact, the flowering periods of fruit trees are not fixed precisely or rigidly, and flowering will depend, to some degree, on location and seasonal conditions. This means that there is some leeway, but to improve the opportunity for pollination varieties should still be selected from adjacent groups. This should mean that the later flowers from the first group will still be producing pollen when the first flowers from the next group start opening, and so on. By careful selection of varieties from across the different flowering groups, you could have a garden full of fruit blossom for a long period through the spring, with each group pollinating the next.

The flowering group should be shown clearly on the growers' label attached to the tree when you buy it. If it does not, ask for advice.

It is rare for a soft fruit to have particular pollination requirements. Most are self-fertile, which means that you will get fruit from just one plant. The exception to this is the blueberry, which is self-fertile to some degree, but the size of the crop and the quality of the fruit will be greatly improved if you grow two different varieties, which will cross-pollinate.

Location and Space

Where to plant and how much space is available are both factors in making the best choice for your garden. Given light and water, most tree fruit will grow perfectly well in most garden situations, taking what nutrients they need from whatever is available in the soil. But fruit growers naturally want to make sure that, wherever possible, their trees are given the best chance to produce a good crop of quality fruit. Like most plants, fruit trees will benefit from an open sunny position. They will grow perfectly well with shade at some time during the day, but sun is essential to promote full ripening of the fruit and, whenever possible, the tree should be positioned to benefit from

the sun. If a choice of sites is available, it would be better if the tree was in the sun later in the day, and in some shade during the morning. This will avoid the potential problem of flowers being 'burned' in frosty conditions by the early morning sun falling on the frozen blossoms.

Fully grown apple trees can take up a lot of space.

If a row of trees or cordons is to be planted, it would be ideal to plant the row running north–south as this will allow the sun to reach both sides of the trees, which will help to balance growth and ripening. Try to avoid planting rows running east–west as this will

Space can always be found in a garden for a few fruit trees.

OPPOSITE: **Apple trees will still fruit with some shade.**

expose one side to the sun much more than the other side; it will also cast a dark shadow behind the row, which will limit what else you can grow there.

Space is less of an issue for soft fruits as the plants tend to be smaller than fruit trees, and they are more adaptable to container growing. As a result, you can grow a wider range in a much smaller space – even the smallest garden could produce 'five-a-day' soft fruits for the family.

Form

In practice, a tree may simply have to be sited in whatever space is available. The decision then is what shape do you want the tree to be, and how big do you want it to grow?

The shape and size of tree that you want will determine how you train and prune the tree. Options include:

Standard/Half-standard: the natural and 'traditional' shape for a tree, like a lollipop, with a bare trunk and a mass of branches radiating out from the top of the trunk. These are very large, full size trees, 3.7m to over 4.5m (12ft to over 15ft), which will dominate a garden, grown on vigorous rootstocks.

Starting with a maiden tree on a vigorous rootstock: for a half-standard, the main stem should be winter pruned at about 1.2–1.4m (4–4ft 6in), to encourage the development of the main branches from this height; for a standard tree, the main stem should be winter pruned at 1.8–2m (6–6ft 6in). The following winter the leader will again be pruned to these

Standard apple tree shape.

heights, the laterals that you want to form the head of the tree being cut back by about half the new growth, to an outward-facing bud. This will encourage the branches to grow upwards and outwards. In future winters, select the branches that you want to keep – these should be the strongest four or five, well spaced, and growing in all directions from the central trunk – and prune them back by about one-third of the new growth to an outward-facing bud. Remove any weak or spindly growth that is not growing in the direction that you want. Keep the trunk clear by removing any laterals that grow out from below the head of the tree. Stake the tree well until the trunk is strong enough to support it. In subsequent years winter prune for shape, to keep the tree tidy and to stimulate vigorous new growth. Summer prune for fruit, according to the type of fruit tree that is being grown. Note that plum trees should not be pruned in the winter as this can lead to infection entering the pruning cuts, so leave

Apple growing as a bush tree.

the formative pruning of plum trees until late spring, when the tree should be in growth.

Bush tree: shaped like a small tree, but kept much shorter, by the use of a dwarfing rootstock and regular maintenance pruning to keep its shape and size in check. Depending on the rootstock, bush and dwarf bush trees can be grown from 1.2–3m (4–10ft) or to a height that is manageable in your situation. This is the initial shape of most fruit trees that are bought from garden centres. As they grow, the object is to develop an open cup-shaped canopy of branches at a width and height that suits the space available and the reach of the grower for picking the fruit.

Dwarf bush trees: these can be grown from maiden trees by pruning the leader down to 60–75cm (24–30in) in its first winter. This should stimulate the growth of several lateral branches from below the pruning cut. During the second winter the laterals are pruned back by about one-third to an outward-facing bud; the aim is to have four or five laterals radiating out from the main stem like spokes on a wheel. Remove any that are weak or poorly spaced (which could lead to overcrowding in the future). Any vigorously growing upright in the centre of the bush should be pruned back to about the height of the original pruning cut. As the laterals grow each year and turn into branches, the shape of the bush is maintained through winter pruning, removing about one-third of the new season's growth and anything that is crossing over. The height is controlled by pruning to the overall size required for the tree. Summer prune for fruit, according to the type of fruit tree that is being grown. As with standard trees, plum trees should not be pruned in the winter. Stake the bush tree well until the trunk is strong enough to support it, which could be lifelong, depending on the rootstock.

Spindlebush: this form of growing is used mainly for apples, and results in a pointed, cone-shaped tree, 1.8–2.1m (6–7ft) tall; it has a central stem, with branches starting low to the ground, from about 60cm (2ft). A spindlebush may look somewhat scruffy and irregular, but is favoured by many fruit growers because it is very efficient, in terms of the quantity of fruit that can be produced in a relatively small space. Also, the quality is usually good as the shape of the tree exposes the maximum amount of fruit to the sun; the cone shape means that the branches are shorter higher up, so they do not overshadow the fruit on the lower branches. The size of the spindlebush also means that picking can usually be done from ground level, without the need for ladder.

Pruning for a spindlebush tree must start with a 'well feathered' maiden tree (that is, one with lots of laterals), on a dwarfing or semi-dwarfing rootstock. After planting, the first winter prune should take the leader down to about 90cm (3ft), and cut the laterals back by about half their length to a downward-pointing bud – the aim is to get these laterals to grow out from the main stem as horizontally as possible, parallel

to the ground. Remove any that are lower than about 60cm (2ft). Through the next spring and summer, as the laterals put on new growth, encourage them to stay horizontal by tying them down gently – the reason for this is that horizontal growth results in the production of more fruiting buds along the branch, and consequently more fruit. Meanwhile, the central leader will be growing: prune this back by about one-third in the second winter, to a bud on the other side to the direction that it has been growing – this should help it continue to grow more or less upright. Leave the horizontally growing laterals, but remove any strong upright growth. In the third winter, again prune back the leader by about one-third, keep the existing laterals tied to the horizontal, and start to trim any laterals that are growing towards the top of the spindlebush, so that they are shorter than the lower

Spindlebush form.

laterals. By the fourth winter the tree will have probably reached its final height, so future pruning will consist of cutting back the central leader to a convenient height, and keeping the higher laterals trimmed, removing any that prove to be too vigorous, and any vertical growth. This form of tree must remain staked throughout its life, and care must be taken to check the ties both on the main stake and on the laterals each year, to make sure they are not cutting into the bark and restricting the flow of sap.

Restricted Forms

Cordon: a single cordon is a way of growing fruit in a form that does not have branches as such, but is kept as a single leader where the fruit will be borne on spurs or short laterals growing along the length of the cordon. This makes the cordon an ideal way to grow many different varieties of fruit in a relatively small space, as they can be planted very close together – as close as 75cm (30in) for apple and pear cordons, 30–38cm (12–15in) for gooseberries and redcurrants. This is a restricted form of growing fruit, ideal for packing lots of different varieties into a relatively small space. This form of growing allows fruit to be trained, depending on space, into double or even triple cordons (two or three leaders), each bearing fruit. A cordon requires permanent support throughout its life, on canes fixed across wires spaced 60–75cm (24–30in) apart; this could be as a freestanding living fence, or stretched taut across a wall or fence panels. If grown across a wall or fence, the wires should fixed to vine eyes about 15cm (6in) out from the surface; the tree itself should be planted 15–22cm (6–9in) out from the wall or fence. Regular summer pruning is required to maintain fruit production. Cordons are usually grown vertically, or down to an angle of 45° depending on space, the vigour of the particular fruit and rootstock, and the look that you want to achieve in your fruit garden. The 45° 'oblique cordons' are particularly useful as they will grow into a longer cordon, which will produce more fruit within a fixed height, compared with a vertical cordon. *Minarette* or *Ballerina* trees are already trained as single cordons, and

the popular 'step over' form is actually an extreme cordon that has been trained to the horizontal at a low-level height where it is easy to pick the fruit and tend to the pruning.

Cordon apples can be grown close together.

Cordon apples in leaf and fruit.

Espalier: a decorative yet highly productive form of training fruit trees against wires, walls or fences, where the fruit is borne on pairs of horizontal branches that are trained out from the central vertical leader. The decorative nature of espaliers means that to display them to best effect they need space, to show off the branches of flowers and fruit. As with other forms of training, espaliers can be restricted to the space available, for example, to cover a single fence panel, about 1.8m (6ft) wide, with four or five tiers to the top of the fence. However, they will look much better if they can be trained across two panels, making the espalier 3.6m (12ft) across. The final width of the espalier has implications for the planting spacing and the total number of espaliers that can be grown in a given space. There is a huge espalier pear at the National Trust's Anglesey Abbey, Cambridgeshire, which is trained over the end wall of a building that is 6m (20ft) or more wide; this pear has nine tiers, and stands over 7m (24ft) tall.

Espaliers are most suitable for apples and pears, and, once established, espaliers require just summer pruning for fruit. They can be bought ready-made, with two or three tiers already in place, but these tend to be relatively expensive as each tier of fruiting arms represents one year's growth and training in the nursery.

Espaliers can be created from scratch, starting with a maiden tree that has its leader pruned each winter to encourage the development of a succession of well spaced, strong, horizontal tiers. New growth from the leader that is in the wrong place or in the wrong direction for the espalier structure is simply removed. Espaliers must be trained against a permanent structure of posts and wires, spaced 38–45cm (15–18in) apart, perhaps as a freestanding living fence or garden divider; alternatively, the wires could be stretched taut across the surface of a wall or fence. If grown across a wall or fence, the wires should be fixed to vine eyes about 15cm (6in) out from the surface; the tree itself should be planted 15–22cm (6–9in) out from the wall or fence.

Pyramid: essentially, this is a vertical cordon which has several tiers of four or five branches radiating out

Small espalier at Godinton House, Kent.

horizontally from the central leader, and kept at a height which is convenient for picking, from a 1.2m (4ft) high by 76cm (30in) wide dwarf pyramid, to a pyramid that is 2.1–2.4m (7–8ft) high by up to 1m (39in) or more wide, according to the space available. The pyramid form of fruit tree is not readily available from garden centres or nurseries so must be created by the fruit grower. Start with a maiden whip, planted, staked and pruned to a bud at about 50cm (20in) from the ground. The central leader should put on vertical growth during the first summer, and will hopefully develop a number of laterals, radiating out from the main stem – these will form the first tier of the pyramid. Ideally, there should be four or five laterals more or less equally spaced around the tree. In the next winter prune these laterals back to about 25cm (10in) to a downward-pointing bud; encourage horizontal growth by carefully tying down these laterals to the horizontal by placing a loop of soft fabric around each lateral and using garden string pegged down to the ground or weighted down with a brick to hold them in position. The central leader is winter pruned to a bud at about 40cm (15in) up from the first tier of laterals, and on the opposite side to the bud that has grown up this year – this will help to keep the central leader growing straight and vertical. During the next summer any sub-laterals that grow on the first tier should be summer pruned to develop fruiting spurs. The leader is left until the winter, when a second tier of laterals should have developed. These are treated the same as the first tier in their first winter: trimmed to a downward-pointing bud at about 25cm (10in) and tied down to the horizontal. The central leader is again pruned, leaving 40cm (15in) of the new growth. This process is repeated until the leader reaches the final height required, where it can be maintained by cutting back each summer. The length of the laterals, forming the width of the entire plant, can also be maintained by cutting back to the length required each summer. Once developed, pyramids are easy to maintain with regular summer pruning, and are suitable for most tree fruit.

Apple *Katy* grown as a pyramid makes an attractive tree when in fruit.

Fan: possibly the most decorative of the restricted forms of growing fruit trees to be found commonly in British gardens; elsewhere in the world fruit trees are sometimes trained in much more complex shapes and forms. With a fan shape, branches radiate out across wires, walls or fences like the fingers on a hand, from a low-cut central point. A fan shows off the flowers and fruit to great effect and can be used for soft fruit like redcurrants and gooseberries, as well as the full range of tree fruits. Like other restricted forms, fruit tree fans can sometimes be found readymade in garden centres, at a price that reflects the amount of work and time that has been spent training the tree. In the garden a fruit grower can easily create their own fruit tree fan, given time, patience and sufficient space – like

Established fan growing against a wall.

the espalier, a fan will easily cover one fence panel, 1.8m (6ft) across, but will look much better across two panels up to 3.6m (12ft) wide. Fans can also be grown on a frame of posts and wires to create a living fence or a divider between different parts of the garden. The framework for training a fan should be based on a series of horizontal wires stretched across the full width, starting 40cm (15in) from the ground, then at every 15cm (6in) up to the final height. If the fan is to be grown across a wall or fence the wires should be fixed to vine eyes about 15cm (6in) out from the surface; the tree itself should be planted 15–22cm (6–9in) out from the wall or fence.

Pruning for a fan-shaped fruit tree should start with a maiden whip, winter pruned after planting to a bud about 60cm (24in) up from the ground. Ideally there should be a pair of good buds below this pruning

cut, which will grow to form the first two ribs of the fan. Two garden canes should be fixed across the wire framework, one on either side of the top of the pruned maiden, sloping upwards away from the tree at an angle of 45° to the ground. During its first summer the pruned maiden should develop a pair of laterals on either side of the main stem, from the buds which were left; these will form the first two ribs of the fan. When these two laterals are about 45cm (18in) long they must be tied gently to the garden canes fixed across the wires. Any vertical growth from the central leader should be pruned right back to the original pruning cut, and any other laterals that develop should be removed – the aim is to have a Y-shaped plant tied to the canes. During the next winter prune back the two lateral ribs to a bud at about 30–45cm (12–18in) from the main stem. During the next sum-

Newly formed fan.

mer continue to tie the new growth from the first two ribs to the canes; at the same time, select strong-growing laterals from the top of the first rib, spaced about 10–15cm (4–6in) apart, and one or two growing downwards, and tie these to canes on the wire framework to form the next set of ribs for the fan. Any laterals growing back towards the wall or fence should be rubbed out and removed as soon as they are spotted; any laterals growing straight out from the face of the fan should be summer pruned back, leaving just one leaf. This training is repeated each year until the fan covers the space available. The main difficulty with fan training is the natural tendency for trees to try to grow vertically upwards, so any strong vertical growth should be removed or it will become dominant and take over the fan, making it lopsided and out of balance.

Rootstocks and the Size of Fruit Tree

Most fruit trees are produced by budding or grafting a named variety onto a rootstock, the part of the tree that is planted into the ground; it is the rootstock that determines the size and vigour of the particular variety of fruit that is growing on the top of the tree. In addition to size and vigour, the rootstock will also have some bearing on how many years it will take before the tree starts to produce fruit, and to some extent the size of the fruit that is grown. Different rootstocks suit different growing conditions: some have particular soil or cultivation requirements to grow at their best, while some may have particular needs in the way they are supported or trained.

How large and how quickly a fruit tree will grow will

Union between rootstock and variety.

be determined to a great extent by the rootstock onto which your chosen fruit has been budded or grafted. The rootstock will also have a bearing on how easy or not it is to train the tree into the form that you want it to take – a vigorous rootstock will quickly outgrow a restricted form, while a dwarfing rootstock will never put on the growth required for a larger tree or bush, and will always remain a weak-looking specimen.

If you cannot decide, or you have no choice in the rootstock, just bear in mind that the descriptions 'vigorous' or 'dwarfing' have been based on how the trees will perform in perfect soil and perfect growing conditions. A vigorous rootstock in thin, poor soil may struggle but will probably grow into a decent tree. A dwarfing rootstock in the same poor conditions may survive, but it will not grow, it will look stunted and

A well-stocked garden centre.

Mail order catalogues are a good way of finding a range of different fruits.

Look for rootstock information on labels.

its fruit will be small in size and few in number. My advice is to look for a tree on a rootstock that suits your ground and your requirements for training; failing that, then go for a more vigorous rootstock. You can always control the size and shape of a tree on a vigorous rootstock through effective pruning, but you will never be able to inject any vigour into a dwarfing rootstock that does not grow into the shape and size that you want, and this will be disappointing.

Most garden centres stock fruit trees that suit the 'average' garden – if there is such a thing; they will grow into average-sized trees and produce some fruit without too much trouble. Fruit trees bought from reputable sources should have the rootstock listed on the label attached to the plant; if you cannot identify the rootstock, move on and buy one that you can identify.

Rootstock selection is not a problem for soft fruits as they tend to be grown on their own roots, and the size of the cordon or bush is very much determined by how active the fruit grower is with the secateurs. With soft fruits, the plants can be trimmed to fit the space available, and a reasonable fruit crop is still possible.

With so many different mouth-watering fruits available to grow, and a well-stocked garden centre, nursery or mail order fruit catalogue, it is easy to get carried away and buy the first tree you see of the variety you have chosen. However, once you have decided on the types and varieties of fruit that you want to grow, it is worth checking that you buy trees on the rootstock that is right for the space and conditions of your garden or wherever you intend to plant and grow the fruit trees. If you buy a tree on a rootstock that is not right for your situation, you could find that it quickly outgrows the space available and becomes unmanageable, or conversely, that it remains small and weak, needs constant attention, is prone to disease and only produces small fruit.

Rootstocks are identified by numbers or names which bear no relationship to tree size in absolute terms or in relation to one another. In fact, absolutes are very difficult when trying to describe the performance of different rootstocks – there are just so many variables – the variety, the soil it is growing in, how much water it receives, how much nutrient it is given, the weather, the training and pruning regime. As a general observation, remember that while vigour and growth can be managed by pruning, you will never be able to inject vigour into a tree that is restricted by a dwarfing rootstock.

The following tables give a general description and a list of features about the most widely available rootstocks used for the most popular fruit trees. If you have any doubts, buy from a reputable nursery or garden centre, and ask for advice before you buy.

APPLE		
Rootstock	General description	Features
M27	Very dwarfing Pyramid, centre leader tree	Height 1.2–1.8m (4–6ft), spread up to 1.5m (5ft) when mature and grown in ideal conditions – good soil and lots of attention to cultivation will be required; must be grown in clean soil, will not tolerate competition from grass or weeds; must be watered regularly in dry periods; small all over and fruits will always be on the small size, but this can be overcome to some extent by thinning; often recommended for container growing, but with little new growth each year, tree will always be thin and weak, giving a stunted appearance; permanent staking required as tree can get top heavy. Fruiting from second or third year. Spacing, 1.2m.
M9	Dwarfing Pyramid, centre leader, bush, cordon, step over	Height 1.8–2.4m (6–8ft), spread 2.7m (9ft) when mature and grown in ideal conditions; will reach full height after about five years; good size fruit; reputedly the most widely planted rootstock in commercial orchards in Britain; brittle roots mean that it must be staked securely throughout its life; needs good soil and clean, weed-free cultivation. Fruiting from second or third year. Spacing, 2.5m.
M26	Semi-dwarfing Pyramid, centre leader, bush, cordon, espalier	Height 2.2–3m (7–10ft). Slightly stronger growing than M9; will grow well in average garden soil, but needs permanent staking on light soils; can be grown in grass. Fruiting from second or third year. Spacing, 3m.
MM106	Semi-vigorous/ semi-dwarfing Pyramid, centre leader, bush, cordon, espalier, fans	Height 4–4.5m (13–14ft). Semi-vigorous on rich soils, semi-dwarfing on poor soils; grows rapidly in early years; good all rounder; can be grown in grass. Fruiting from second or third year.
M25	Very vigorous Full grown standard	Height 3.7m to over 4.5m (12ft to over 15ft). For large, standard trees, as found in many traditional orchards; grows successfully in a wide range of soils and in grass. Heavy cropper, comes into fruit bearing early in its life.

PEARS		
Rootstock	**General description**	**Features**
Quince C	Dwarfing Cordon, espalier, fan	Height 2.4–3m (8–10ft). Rapid growth in early years, comes into cropping quickly, then growth slows; requires very fertile soil and permanent support; best suited for vigorous varieties growing on good soils. Should fruit from second or third year.
Quince A	Semi-dwarfing Cordon on poor soil, espalier, fan	Height 3–3.6m (10–12ft). Vigorous enough for most garden situations; recommended for general garden use. Should fruit from third or fourth year.
BA29	Semi-vigorous Bush, semi-standard	Height 4.5m (15ft) in good soil. Will tolerate dry soils.

PLUMS & GAGES		
Rootstock	**General description**	**Features**
Pixy	Semi-dwarfing Bush, dwarf pyramid, cordon	Height 2.4–3m (8–10ft). Small root system: needs support, good soil and irrigation to thrive; some resistance to bacterial canker; fruit size smaller than Saint Julien A. Fruiting in three years.
Saint Julien A	Semi-vigorous Bush, fan, half standard, standard	Height 3–4.5m (10–15ft). Good for general garden use, enough vigour to get established without too much trouble. Fruits in fourth or fifth year.

CHERRY		
Rootstock	**General description**	**In practice**
Tabel	Very dwarfing Container growing, small bush.	Height 2.5–3m (8–10ft).
Gisela 5	Dwarfing Container growing, bush, fan	Height 3–4m (10–13ft). Needs fertile soil. Fruits in second or third year.
Colt	Semi-vigorous Bush, half-standard, pyramid, fan	Height up to 8m (27ft) but can be restricted to 3.6-5m (12–16ft) pruning. Will grow in a wide range of soils; some resistance to bacterial canker. Fruits early, in third year; good sized fruit produced from third or fourth year.

PEACH		
Rootstock	**General description**	**In practice**
Pixy	Semi-dwarfing	Height 2.4–3m (8–10ft).
Saint Julien A	Semi-vigorous	Height 3–3.5m (10–12ft).

APRICOTS		
Rootstock	**General description**	**In practice**
Torinel	Semi-vigorous	Final height 2.4–3m (8–10ft). Fruits in three years.
Saint Julien A	Semi-vigorous	3–4m (10–13ft).

PLANNING AND PREPARING THE GARDEN FOR FRUIT

New Garden

Preparing the Site and the Soil

In a perfect world, fruit would be grown in deep, rich, fertile soil that is well irrigated and weed-free, on a site that is warm and sunny in the spring and summer, cold enough to provide the necessary period of winter chill, yet frost-free at blossom time – but few fruit growers are lucky enough to enjoy such luxury. Most of us have to make the best of the situation that we find in our gardens.

When choosing a site for growing fruit, bear in mind that the fruit trees and bushes are likely to be there for quite a long time – with the possible exception of strawberries, fruits are not like herbaceous perennials that can be moved and split without too much bother and will recover quickly from the ordeal.

Tree fruits can be grown in the open or against walls or fences that face east, west or south – fruit trees may grow against north-facing walls, but without sun to ripen the fruit it will never achieve full flavour or sweetness. The exception to this is acid cherries, which will ripen to some degree if north-facing, but this does not mean that this is the preferred situation.

Fruit grown in the open would ideally be in rows that run north–south, so that each side of the plants receives an equal amount of sunlight and shade. Try to avoid running rows east–west as this exposes only the south-facing side to the sun, and creates heavy shade

OPPOSITE PAGE: **Strawberries grow well in containers.**

behind the rows that will affect the row behind (and anything else trying to grow in that area).

In practice, fruit may have to fit in with the existing layout of the site, and be grown in-line with paths, fences or other permanent features of the garden. This is not necessarily a problem as some shade during the day is not likely to cause too many problems for fruit in respect of ripening. In fact, during the increasingly hot summers of recent years gooseberries, which are essentially woodland fruit, and even some apples, have been scorching in the intense heat of the sun in the late afternoon – in this situation, shade is a great benefit to the plants and their fruit.

Irrigation is another factor to consider about the site – will the ground provide sufficient water for the fruit, and how easy will it be to irrigate if necessary. This issue is not exclusive to fruit, of course, and any gardener will need to consider this, whatever they are growing. Rainwater saved in water butts is most valuable and comes at no cost compared with mains water, which is increasingly being metered; 'grey water' (that is, waste water from washing up, baths or showers) can also be used for irrigating established fruit, but is probably best avoided on strawberries, where it could contaminate the fruit itself.

The exact opposite to the need for irrigation is where the site becomes waterlogged. This may not be a problem for fruit such as blackcurrants, which will tolerate some degree of waterlogging, but new plantings could be damaged as the roots will not be able to access sufficient oxygen, and they will just sit and rot in waterlogged soil. Land drains can be used, but in a domestic garden the problem could be tackled by

A new fruit garden can be created by removing lawn.

incorporating grit into the soil to aid drainage; as a last resort, try to find a site that does not get waterlogged.

Before planting fruit it is important to clear the ground of perennial weeds, such as couch grass, dock, bindweed, horse-tail, etc., which will be difficult to remove once they are entangled in the roots of fruit trees. Annual weeds are not such a problem and can be dealt with easily by cultivation and hand selection when they appear. It is tempting to use weed-killers or herbicides to clear the ground, but there is a risk that residues from these chemicals could linger in the soil and affect the growth of the trees and bushes that

you plant; the residues may even find their way into the fruit which we then eat. Even glyphosate, which is reputed to be neutralized once it hits the soil and therefore safe to use, has been reported by some fruit growers to cause problems with the growth and development of their fruit. One effective way to deal with weeds over a large area is to cover the ground with

LEFT: **Some situations can prove difficult for fruit.**

RIGHT: **A water butt is a great way to save valuable rain water.**

Strips of wild flowers growing in the orchard at RHS Garden Wisley, Surrey.

an impermeable barrier such as black polythene or old carpeting – this will exclude the light and emerging weeds will not be able to develop. This, of course, will not happen overnight and it is only feasible if the ground is not needed for a year or so. It may be hard work, but the safest and most effective method of weed control is the physical removal of the weed.

As in most areas of gardening, there are exceptions. Strips of wild flower meadow grown near fruit trees and bushes are a positive advantage – they provide a nectar bar for pollinating insects and a safe home for natural predators that will help to control pests on the fruit. One 'weed' that can be beneficial to fruit growers is feverfew (*Tanacetum parthenium*): some fruit growers report that growing this strong-smelling herb around gooseberries discourages the adult gooseberry sawfly, and thus reduces damage to the plants and the need for drastic pest control.

When planting fruit trees into grass, an area of about 1m (39in) across should be removed for each

tree so that the grass does not compete with the fruit. Generally, in a garden situation, it is not a good idea to allow weeds or grass to grow up under fruit bushes or close to the trunks of fruit trees as they will use up water and valuable nutrients, which will then not be available for the fruit. Also, they may harbour pests such as aphids, or create a microclimate that encourages fungal growth that could attack the tree.

Having cleared the site of weeds, dig over the soil and break up any large lumps of clay. Double-digging, that is digging to twice the depth of a spade and turning over the underlying soil, will certainly benefit fruit trees as they will be able to get their roots down that much more quickly and soil drainage will be improved, reducing the problem of waterlogging. If you already have a good depth of topsoil over clay, try not to bring too much clay up to the surface as it will tend to dry out quickly and develop a hard, impenetrable layer that is all too familiar in gardens made up of heavy clay. Light, sandy soils will benefit greatly from the

When planting into grass leave a clear space around the tree.

incorporation of plenty of compost to add organic matter to the soil and help retain moisture. Most fruit will also benefit from a light application of well-rotted farmyard manure, and the incorporation of a slow-acting, long-term fertilizer like 'blood, fish and bone' into the soil used to back-fill the hole and around the roots when planting.

Part of the preparation will be working out what support the fruit will need when it is planted, and throughout its productive life. For single fruit trees and bushes this could be as simple as using a wooden stake or a garden cane for support, depending on the size of the plant. Cane fruits, or restricted forms of fruit tree, will need wires stretched between posts or across the face of a wall or fence for support. It is always much easier to install wires or supports before the fruit

is planted, as it is much easier to work in an area that is not overgrown with plants, and the likelihood of causing damage to existing plants is reduced.

Established Fruit Garden

Improvement and Renovation

Fruit growing is not all about planting up new orchards or new beds of strawberries – many gardens will already have some fruit plants which, with a bit of care and attention, can be reinvigorated and brought back into worthwhile production.

IMPROVING AN EXISTING FRUIT GARDEN

The first thing to do is to take a good look at the plant:

- do the leaves look healthy – are they a good green colour, are they damaged by pests?
- is there any new growth – always a good sign, or is it weak and suffering from virus or disease?
- is there any evidence of fruit – mummi-fied on the branches, or on the ground beneath?
- are there any dead patches or dead branches that need to be removed?
- has it outgrown its site and situation?
- is it the shape and size that you want?
- do you want this kind of fruit growing where it is?

Take a good look at the branches of established trees.

Remove any dead or dying branches.

There may be other considerations, but all things being equal it is worth trying to renovate old plants and get some fruit for free, or at least without the cost of buying new stock. Renovation is best done in the winter when the plant is dormant (apart from with plum trees, when the cutting of wood is best left until growth starts in the spring). Failing that, try to carry out renovation work in the early spring. This will give the plant a chance to put on new growth that will mature before the onset of winter. If left much later, any new growth could be damaged during the cold winter months.

The first thing to do is to clear the soil around the base of the plant, removing any weeds. This will help you get a good view of the plant and make it easier to get close to work on it. Remove any dead or dying branches, cutting back to living healthy wood, which will show green beneath the bark. On branches and laterals try to cut back to just above a healthy bud, and avoid leaving stubs (short, bare lengths of a branch left above a bud after pruning), as the short length that is left is likely to die back, will not produce any more buds and may become a host for fungal infections such as coral spot, which can affect the rest of the branch.

This done, consider whether the remaining branches look overcrowded or badly spaced. If so, remove a proportion of these, up to a maximum of one-third in any one year, to leave a well balanced plant. Shorten the branches to a convenient length that is in proportion to the plant or that fits in with the form or training that you want for the plant.

Cane fruits should have all of the old canes that have borne fruit in previous years removed, leaving just the new growth from last year, or anything new that is coming up.

Old blackcurrants can be pruned quite severely, removing up to one-third of the old branches to ground level. In extremis, blackcurrants can be cut entirely to the ground; if fed and watered sufficiently, they will throw up new growth in the current year, which should bear fruit the following year.

On trees or bushes where the fruit is formed on spurs, look at the spur systems. Are they short and full of fruit buds, or have they been allowed to grow too long to be manageable and productive. If they look too long, treat them as laterals and prune back to a good, healthy looking bud that is about 10cm (4in) from the branch in the case of tree fruits, or 5cm (2in) for soft fruits.

Step back and take a good look – is the fruit tree or bush now a better shape and size, with nothing that

Spur system on pear.

is dead or dying? If not, perform the final bit of trimming until it is right for the plant and the situation.

Next it is time to feed the plant by feeding the soil. Fork round the plant to loosen the soil, taking care not to damage any surface roots. Sprinkle a general-purpose fertilizer round the root area and fork it in gently. This could be something like *Growmore*, *Vitax Q4* or a pelleted poultry manure, at the rate recommended on the packet by the manufacturer – there is no point exceeding this rate, and excess may do more harm than good. Well-composted farmyard manure is a useful alternative. Mulch the root area with a good depth of garden compost, up to 10cm (4in), but be sure to keep it away from the trunk or stem.

Finally, give the plant a good water, through the mulch. Water regularly, especially in times of drought, until the plant shows signs that all this care and attention has paid off and new growth has started. The water can be laced with a seaweed-based feed, which will help replace missing nutrients; this could even be applied as a foliar feed, which will get the nutrients into the plant much more quickly than a root drench.

However, if all this fails, and there are no signs of improvement and no fruit to reward all the effort,

Removing a plum tree suffering badly from bacterial canker.

it is time to think about whether the plant is worth keeping. This is not a decision to take lightly, and it may not all hinge on whether fruit is being produced. A fruit tree has many other reasons for staying in a garden, whether it fruits or not – it may look good, flowering and providing a background to the garden, or it may hide something worse that will be exposed if it is removed; it may be a rare or unusual variety that needs to be protected; it will certainly be providing a habitat for wildlife, principally for birds but also for insects that provide food for the birds, and it may even be a roost for bats – in which case its removal would be an offence against the Wildlife and Countryside Act and the Habitats regulations.

If there are no other considerations and the tree is removed, avoid planting fruit of the same type in the same place as any soil-borne diseases or nutritional deficiencies in the site will adversely affect the new tree. This can be overcome to some degree by the complete removal of the old soil along with the tree, and its replacement with new soil, but this requires a great deal of work.

Old cane fruit may not be worth renovating as they may be suffering from a virus, which would continue to weaken the plant; in this case removal is the only option. Similarly, strawberries start to deteriorate after three or four years so are hardly worth renovating – it would be best to dig them up and start somewhere fresh with new plants.

Container Growing – A Worthwhile Option

The concept of growing fruit in containers comes as a surprise to many gardeners, who tend to associate containers with decorative annuals or bulbs, but the principle is not new and was practised widely by Victorian fruit growers. Whole books were written, and conferences and exhibitions organized in the nineteenth century so that fruit growers could show off their skills, or the skills of their gardeners, in managing to grow fruit in containers. One factor that makes container growing so much easier for fruit growers today has been the development of dwarfing rootstocks which produce naturally smaller fruit trees and bushes, which are more convenient to manage in containers.

There are many advantages to growing fruit in containers: they are portable, so can be brought under cover if frost threatens the blossom, or moved if a sunnier position is required to aid fruit ripening; and water, fertilizer and nutrients can be concentrated where they are required – on the roots – which helps avoid the problems of excessive or insufficient feeding, and helps conserve the use of precious water, placing it where it can do the most good. Container-grown fruit can also be extremely decorative, so it is ideal for filling a gap in a border or a blank space on a patio.

A range of fruit growing in containers at RHS Garden Wisley, Surrey.

Containers come in all shapes and sizes.

Choice of Container

Containers come in many different shapes, sizes and materials. The size should be sufficient to contain the roots of the plant without damage or distortion, and allowing enough space for a season or two's growth. Consider the shape and size of the plant, and choose a container that will be stable and heavy enough to remain upright in windy conditions. There is often a temptation to choose a container that is overlarge, thinking that this will give the roots plenty of space to grow, and will avoid the need to re-pot for a few years. This is a mistake, as the plant may simply put on root

growth until it fills the container, at the expense of top growth or fruit. Also, the excess compost will lose its nutrients and tend to go sour over time, which will not help the plant. This is also an issue when moving the plant on from one container to another – as a general rule-of-thumb, for containers up to about 45cm (18in) across, just increase the size by 3–5cm (1.25–2in) on either side of the rootball, or just about enough to get a hand down each side. For large containers, use your judgement and pick a container that will allow a worthwhile amount of fresh compost to be added, without looking overlarge in proportion to the rootball.

Materials

Unglazed terracotta pots: the traditional flower pot. They have several advantages: they look good; being porous, they allow the roots to get oxygen, which helps them to grow and develop; and they tend to keep the roots cooler than other materials, which is useful in hot conditions, through the natural effects of evaporating water. The downsides are that they are heavy, and therefore difficult to manoeuvre; water evaporates rapidly from unglazed terracotta, which means that they require watering more frequently if they stand in direct sunlight; and they are prone to frost damage, especially if frozen when wet. (Despite the 'frost resistant' properties that some manufacturers claim for them, most are made in countries that are not subject to the freezing conditions experienced in British winters, and frost damage often occurs.) Replacement can be expensive and time-consuming.

Glazed terracotta: these pots have many of the positive benefits of unglazed pots, plus they will not dry out so quickly, and are better protected from frost damage as water does not enter the body of the material. The main problem is the weight of glazed terracotta pots, which can make them difficult to move, and they can also be expensive.

Plastic: not always as attractive as terracotta, but certainly more functional, plastics are much lighter and therefore easier to move than terracotta, and are good at retaining water. The large black plastic 'nursery tubs' available from 30 litres to 150 litres have strong, thick walls and usually a pair of sturdy handles; these are ideal for fruit, especially tree fruits – they may not be the most attractive containers but they are extremely functional, and they can always be 'hidden' inside more decorative glazed pots. The thin black plastic pots used by the nursery and garden centre trade are quite useful; they are strong and cheap to buy, and again they can be placed inside more decorative pots. However, although they retain moisture quite well, the impervious plastic means that the plant roots cannot 'breathe', and there is a greater danger of rotting; also the plastic walls heat up quickly in direct sunlight, and can overheat the roots – this is a particular problem for plants in small black pots.

Metal: increasingly fashionable, and therefore more popular, in recent years, metal containers may look attractive but they have one distinct disadvantage for growing plants – they absorb heat from the sun very readily, and can heat up to temperatures that can damage the roots of plants and burn anyone who happens to touch the hot metal container with bare flesh. They should be avoided for fruit growing.

Planting the Container

When re-potting a plant, first soak it in water in preparation for the move, then remove it carefully from the old container, without damaging the roots. Keep the rootball covered with damp sacking or a polythene sheet to prevent the roots from drying out. Remove any old crocks or drainage material from the underside of the rootball. Inspect for vine weevil grubs – if any are found, they should be dealt with accordingly and any old compost removed, as it will inevitably be harbouring more grubs. If the rootball is very pot-bound, with the roots winding tightly round the inside of the old container, gently tease out some of the roots, taking care not to break any. Add drainage materials at the base of the new container, and a layer of fresh compost. Place the plant into the centre of the new container and hold it upright while you fill-in around the roots with fresh compost; add a long-term/slow-acting balanced fertilizer, such as *Vitax Q4*, according to the manufacturer's instructions. Continue filling the container with compost, shaking it around the roots, and firming down to remove any air pockets. The aim is to keep the plant at the same depth in the new compost as it was in the old compost. The final level of the compost should be several centimetres down from the top of the container so that sufficient water can be given to the plant to soak the rootball without it overflowing the container. If the plant needs support, add garden canes or stakes into the container, trying to avoid damage to the roots, and secure the plant as required. Water well to make sure that the new compost is washed around the roots. Top up the container with compost if it sinks down after watering. Leave the re-potted plant in a shady place for a few days to get over the experience, before moving to its final position.

Composts

Ready-mixed composts for container gardening are widely available in most garden centres, 'and these are perfect for most plants. However, the use of a loam-based compost to fill a large container will tend to make it very heavy, and it may be so dense that water-

ing and drainage may prove problematic. Conversely, a container filled exclusively with a soilless multipurpose compost could give problems of stability as it is so light, and it will tend to dry out more quickly, meaning that it must be watered more frequently.

A good compromise for growing most fruit in containers is a 50:50 mix of loam-based compost, such as John Innes No. 2, and a soilless multipurpose compost, with horticultural grit added to make sure it has sufficient drainage.

If cane fruit such as raspberries are to be grown in a container, the loam-based compost could be reduced to 20 per cent, and for the remaining 80 per cent use a multipurpose compost, ericaceous for preference; again add some grit to aid drainage.

Strawberries will grow happily in multipurpose compost, as found in most growing bags. But if you

Ready mixed composts for containers are widely available.

are planting strawberries in pots or other containers, the addition of some loam-based compost (ideally a 50:50 mixture) and grit will improve the structure of the compost and reduce the amount of watering that will need to be done.

Fruit that has been growing in containers for some years will need to have the compost refreshed and reinvigorated from time to time, and perhaps the plant moved to a larger container. This is best done during the dormant period, the winter months. Carefully remove the plant, inspecting the roots and dealing with any pests such as vine weevil grubs, and replace the old compost completely with fresh compost mixed with a slow-release fertilizer. Make sure that the compost is at the same level as it was before re-potting. An alternative would be to top-dress the container by removing the top few centimetres of compost, taking care not to damage the roots, and replacing what has been removed with fresh compost and the slow-release fertilizer – but this method does not allow for the inspection of the roots for pests. Care must be taken to ensure that the compost level is the same as it was, and that there is sufficient space at the top of the container for watering.

Watering

Plants growing in containers are totally reliant on the fruit grower for water. They may receive some when it rains, but a plant in full leaf acts like an umbrella and even after a heavy downpour the compost in the container may be relatively dry.

If watering from the top, there should be enough space between the compost and the top of the container to enable you to give it a good soak. It is better to fill the container with water up to the rim, to wet the compost through, rather than watering a little each day.

Avoid the temptation to over-water as this will lead to stagnant compost, to the detriment of the plant. Try to use rainwater if it is available; mains water will suffice but the mineral salts it contains may leach through porous terracotta containers and leave an unattractive white residue on the surface. (This can

be removed with a stiff brush.) Grey water is valuable in the garden for watering into the soil, but when used for containers it may build up undesirable deposits of soaps or phosphates in the compost so should only be used as a last resort.

Containers that have dried out will be difficult to water from the top, as the water will not be able to penetrate the hard surface and the water will simply run down the inside of the container and out through the drainage holes. A better method is to dunk the entire container into water; a large round plastic garden trug is particularly useful for this, as they have relatively low sides, about 40cm (16in), which means that the planted container does not need to be lifted up too high, and two handles, which makes them easy to manoeuvre when full of water. Don't leave the container submerged for too long, as this will prevent oxygen getting to the plant roots and will effectively drown the roots.

Stand the container in a saucer to save and conserve any excess water that runs out through the container.

Feeding

Incorporate a slow-release fertilizer in the compost when mixing. Adding a dilute liquid feed each week when watering during the growing season, perhaps as a 'Sunday treat', ensures that the plant has sufficient nutrients when it needs them – it is easy to wash nutrients out of the compost when watering containers. Switch to a weekly feed with a high potash tomato fertilizer once the fruit has set.

Berried Fruit

Gooseberries and redcurrants are well suited for container growing, and can be pruned or trained in proportion to the size of the container used. They may be kept as small bushes, or grown as single cordons to take up less space; a particularly effective display can be produced if they are grown as standards, and the fruit becomes easy to pick as it hangs down below the branches. Make sure that the roots have sufficient room, and that the container is kept watered but not waterlogged. For best results use a 50:50 mixture of soil-based potting compost, such as John Innes no. 2, and a multipurpose compost, with some grit added to improve drainage. Fruit in containers will need feeding more than fruit in the ground, as the nutrients will be washed out through the container as it is watered.

Blackcurrants can also be grown in containers, using the same 50:50 compost mix; do not forget the grit to improve drainage. Container-grown blackcurrants will also need regular feeding and top-dressing, and, unless the container is large, it can be difficult to keep up the cultivation regime that encourages replacement branches from the base of the plant, and the fruit crop will be small.

Cane Fruit

Growing raspberries in large containers has become popular in recent years, and is a system that has been adopted by some pick-your-own farms. Container growing is particularly suitable for primocane autumn-fruiting raspberries as they fruit on the new canes grown each season, so there are fewer canes to deal with. The container should be relatively large, 40–50cm (16–20in) across the top, 50 litres or more, to allow for the development of the canes and sufficient watering. For the planting medium, use a mixture of 80 per cent peat-free compost, ericaceous for preference, plus 20 per cent loam-based potting compost, such as John Innes No. 2; add some grit to aid drainage. Make sure that the container is kept watered but

Tom Putt **apple tree on M27 dwarfing rootstock growing in a glazed terracotta pot.**

not waterlogged, and use rainwater if available as this will help keep the compost slightly acid, which is beneficial for raspberries. Fruit in containers will need more feeding than fruit in the ground, as the nutrients will wash out through the container as it is watered, so add a slow-release fertilizer when mixing the compost and water regularly with a high potash tomato fertilizer as soon as the fruits are set. Support the growing and fruiting raspberries with garden string tied to a bamboo cane in the centre of the container, or with garden string tied round a series of bamboo canes pushed in around the edge of the container.

Other cane fruit such as loganberries or blackberries can be grown in containers, but the rampant nature of the growth put on by their canes will require firm control, and they must be tied in to a supporting structure continuously as they grow. This could be a frame mounted in the container itself, or the canes could be trained on wires across an adjacent wall or fence.

Strawberries

For strawberry growers, the choice of containers is limited only by the imagination: garden centres offer a range of towers, patio planters and pot systems for growing strawberries, in addition to the traditional strawberry planter – basically a large pot with holes or moulded pockets around the sides, filled with compost, into which strawberry runners are inserted. Strawberries can also be planted to create a decorative and edible edge to large tubs or containers holding flowers or shrubs. Whichever style of container you choose, the basic requirements for strawberries are the same: they need good-quality compost, regular watering and feeding, and protection from slugs and birds.

Tree Fruit

By choosing varieties grown on a dwarfing rootstock, most tree fruits can be grown successfully in containers. Choose a container that is large enough to take the rootball without damaging the roots, and that will hold sufficient compost to keep the tree fed through several seasons without the need to replace the compost. The container should be in proportion to the shape and size of the tree or bush that is to be grown, and when filled it needs to be heavy enough to prevent the tree being blown over by the wind. Bush and cordon forms are particularly suited to container growing, or the tree could be kept to the shape of a miniature tree with a bare trunk and an array of branches growing from the top; some fruit growers even produce examples of fruiting espaliers in containers. Keep the fruit tree in shape by winter pruning, except for plums which should not be pruned during the winter but left until growth starts in the spring. Tree fruits in containers have the same pollination needs as fruit grown in the ground, and will require the same summer pruning regime to keep producing fruit.

PLANTING, SUPPORT AND PRUNING

Fruit is a long-term crop, and once planted is likely to stay in the same place for many years, the exception being strawberries, which benefit from replacement every three or four years. Because of this longevity, it is worth spending time preparing the soil well and giving some care and attention to the planting.

Planting Techniques

While the planting hole is being prepared, soak the bare roots or the container in water.

Having prepared the site and the soil, look at the container holding the roots of the new fruit plant – this will give an idea of the shape and size of the hole that needs to be dug to take the new plant. In fact, the hole will need to be dug a bit bigger across and a little deeper, to accommodate any compost that is added during planting. Sprinkle the soil that has been removed with 'blood, fish and bone', which is a slow-release, long-term fertilizer that will help the plant develop a strong and healthy root system. Add some compost to the hole and mix it with the soil at the bottom.

When planting any new fruit (with the exception of blackcurrants, which need to be planted lower to encourage new fruiting shoots from beneath the ground), the soil should be kept at the same level as the plant was growing at in the nursery or the container and no deeper, as you do not want to encourage new shoots from below ground level. The same applies to bare-rooted plants – keep the soil at

OPPOSITE PAGE: **Winter pruned redcurrant lateral after pruning.**

the same level that the plant was at in the nursery. For accuracy, lay a garden cane across the top of the hole, resting on the ground on either side, and this will show where the top of the compost around the rootball should line up.

Ready the plant itself by removing it carefully from the packaging or container in which it was bought. It may be that the fruit tree was supplied 'bare rooted' from a nursery and that the roots are just wrapped in damp material, such as hessian, or in a black plastic bag or pot, covered loosely with damp compost. Remove any drainage crocks from the base of container-grown plants. If the roots have outgrown the container and have produced a tight bundle round the inside of the pot, tease out any root tips gently, to encourage growth out and into the garden soil. If this is not done, there is a tendency for the roots to continue growing round and round in a tight knot, and this will mean that the fruit tree will never anchor itself securely in the ground, and watering will be very difficult as all the roots are concentrated in a tight bundle that will be prone to drying out.

At this point the plant will have to be lifted, and it is likely to be quite heavy. Always use safe practice when lifting. Once you have a firm grip on the plant or container, keep your back straight and lift with your legs, not with your back. To lower the heavy plant, again use your legs not your back. Work with a second person or use a barrow or lifting device to move very heavy plants. It is easy to get carried away and start moving heavy plants about without much considera-tion, but safety in the garden is very important.

Lower the plant into the hole – the aim is to posi-tion it upright, with the top of the compost or the soil line on a bare-rooted plant level with the surrounding ground. A garden cane laid across the top of the hole will show this. If the plant is too low, the hole is too deep. Add some soil to the base of the hole to raise it up, and then check again. If the plant is too high, dig out the hole under the plant and check again. Once the plant is in position and upright, start to scoop the garden soil back into the hole. When the hole is about half filled, pour some water into the hole around the rootball; this will wash the loose soil in around the roots and reduce the chance of any air pockets forming under the roots, which will prevent the roots taking up water and nutrients. As the water drains round the roots, continue back-filling with the loose soil. When the filled hole is level with the surrounding garden, water again around the plant; the soil level will drop as it gets washed round the roots. Top up the soil level when the water drains away. At this

point it may help to raise up a ridge of soil in a circle around the new plant, so that it looks as if it has been planted in a saucer – the diameter will depend on the size of the plant, but it will need to be large enough to contain about a can of water without overflowing. The idea is to conserve any water that is given to the new plant. A newly planted fruit tree or bush will require daily watering after planting to help it get established in its new position. In addition, apply a mulch of compost around the new plant to help keep the moisture in the soil, but make sure that the mulch is not in direct contact with the trunk or stem of the plant, as this could provide an entry point for a fungal infection which will kill the plant.

Once planted, most fruit trees and bushes will require some form of support to help them get estab-

Planning is essential for a long-term crop like fruit.

lished and to protect them from wind damage. It is much easier to arrange this at the same time as planting, rather than wait for the plant to grow and potentially get out of hand or damaged before giving it any support and protection.

Check that the roots fit into the prepared hole.

Take a good look at the roots of the new tree before planting.

Place a cane across the hole to check the planting level.

Dig a hole large enough to take the roots without causing damage.

The planting level should be the same as in the nursery.

Start to backfill around the roots.

Top the soil level and raise a ridge of soil around the new plant.

Firm the soil gently around the roots.

Continue to backfill.

'Puddle-in' the roots with water.

Apply mulch.

ABOVE: **The planted tree is now in position.**

BELOW: **Tie it firmly against a stake set at 45 degrees.**

Support

The size and strength of the support (posts, wires, walls, fences, etc.) required will depend to a great extent on the form of growing that has been chosen, the ultimate height and shape of the plant, and the weight of fruit that it is likely to carry. For example, a gooseberry grown as a bush or cordon would be supported adequately by a garden cane; a rambling blackberry will require a series of wires; an apple tree grown as a bush or pyramid will need a strong wooden stake.

For generations garden canes have been used for supporting plants. They are cheap and versatile, and resist rotting for many years without the need to be treated with chemicals. It is always advisable to use new canes, as these will, by definition, last longer. Also new garden canes will be stronger and less brittle than old ones, which means that they are less likely to snap when they are being pushed into the ground. When pushing garden canes into the ground, do not put your full weight on to the cane because if it breaks or gives way you could overbalance, fall, hurt yourself and damage the plant. If the ground is hard, start the hole for the cane with a garden fork – this should reduce the need to push too hard. Put eye protectors on the tops of canes for safety.

Treated wooden stakes and posts come in many shapes sizes; some are round, others square, and they are available in a wide range of lengths. They are likely to have been given a chemical treatment to help resist rot at ground level for a few years, but will need regular inspection to make sure they remain strong enough to support the tree. Choose a stake or post of sufficient size to provide support for a few years' growth — this may mean that initially it looks out of proportion to the young tree that it is supporting. Because of their size, wooden stakes and posts may need to be driven into the ground using a mallet, or sunk into a prepared hole. A metal spike could be knocked into the ground and then removed to provide a pilot hole for the wooden stake.

Depending on the situation and the plant being supported, the garden cane or wooden stake may be fixed vertically to keep the plant upright. The lightness

ABOVE: Choose supports appropriate to the way you plan to grow the fruit.

LEFT: Fruit trees will need a strong wooden stake for support.

Garden canes being used to support a fan-trained peach.

of garden canes means that they can also be fixed at an angle across wires to support fruit that is being grown as an oblique cordon or trained as a fan.

To support newly planted fruit trees that are to be grown upright, in the form of standards, bushes, spindlebushes or pyramids, it would seem natural to fix the stake upright, close to the trunk, and tie the tree to it. Indeed, this method will provide excellent support. There is a danger that driving a stake into the ground near the tree may damage the roots, but with care it will certainly be firm and strong. However, based on the experience of professional fruit growers, it can be more advantageous to fix the stake in the ground away from the base of the tree and set at an angle of 45° to the ground, so that the top of the stake meets the young tree about halfway between the ground and the point where the main branches start to grow. The tree is tied to the stake where they cross. The main advantage of this approach is that the roots are held firm but the top of the tree is allowed to move in the wind, which is said to help the development of strong roots so that the tree will become

Fruit tree supported by stake at 45 degrees to the ground.

established more quickly than if it is held too securely. Tie the tree to the stake using a soft rubber tree-tie or garden twine; the tie should not be too tight and should be checked regularly to make sure that it does not restrict the flow of sap as the tree grows. Likewise, make sure that the tree and the stake do not rub together as this could damage the bark and provide an entry point for disease.

This technique can be used for established trees that need support, where a stake driven into the ground near to the plant is likely to cause root damage. An alternative way of supporting established trees is to use two wooden stakes, fixed upright in the ground, away from the roots, on either side of the fruit tree; then fix a crossbar between the two, to form a 'Π' shape; the tree is then tied to the crossbar using a tree tie.

When tying fruit to canes, use a soft garden twine made from natural materials such as jute. Alternatively, soft plastic ties are available, which will last longer and have the advantage of stretching as the plant grows so they are less likely to damage the bark or cut off the supply of water and nutrients. If using garden twine, first loop the twine around the fruit tree, then cross the twine between the tree and the cane in a figure of eight, loop the twine twice round the cane and tie firmly with a reef knot. Try to finish with the knot resting on the cane rather than on the fruit tree, so that the bark is not rubbed and damaged. The twine

should support the tree and allow for some natural movement, but it must not cut into the bark. Rubber tree ties are good for fixing larger fruit trees to stakes. Whatever material is used, do not forget to check each season that the ties are still supporting the plant effectively. Make sure they are not too tight, and loosen as necessary to prevent damage to the bark and cutting off the supply of water and nutrients.

Never use wire, even plastic-coated wire, to tie directly round the bark of a fruit tree – it will quickly cut into the bark and cause major damage, and could cut off the water supply and kill the plant.

However, wire does play an important part in support and training. In particular, it is the best way to support fruit growing across walls or fence panels. The wire used should be galvanized, to resist rust, and should be at least 1.4mm diameter, sometimes referred to as 17 gauge, to support soft fruit; for tree fruit it is better to use the heavier 1.6mm diameter (16 gauge). Wires used across walls or fence panels will need to be stretched tightly between vine eyes – these are strong metal fixings with a screw thread at one end, to attach to the wooden fence or a wall plug, and a metal loop at the other end, through which the wire is tied. The vine eyes should hold the wires about 15cm (6in) out from the wall or fence, to allow a good flow of air behind the plant; it also makes the tying easier as there will be space between the wires and the fence or wall. Wires across a 1.8m (6ft) panel or

Garden canes, galvanized wire and stout posts supporting trained fruit trees.

space will require a vine eye at each end; wires across wider spaces will need additional vine eyes at intervals to prevent sagging and provide support.

Wires can also be used between upright posts to form the framework for a fruiting fence. When fixing wires to wooden posts, staples can be used rather than vine eyes.

Wires for supporting cordons, or for training cane fruits, are usually started at about 60–75mm (24–30in) up from the ground, and spaced about 60cm (24in) apart, until they reach the desired height, usually the top of the fence or panel. For fan training, start the wires lower down, about 40cm (15in) from the ground, then every 15cm (6in) to the final height. Make sure that the vine eyes hold the wires about 15cm (6in) out from the surface of the wall or fence.

Pruning

It is easy to get obsessive about pruning, as it is often promoted as some kind of 'mystical art' that can only be understood and practised by the fruit-growing cognoscenti. In reality, all pruning amounts to is the organized and controlled cutting of a plant to make the most of its growing and fruiting potential. While pruning is indeed important in fruit growing, it really is not something to worry about too much. Like many skills in the garden, practice may make perfect – the more you practice pruning, the more confident you will become, recognizing where to make each cut for best results. During pruning mistakes may well be made, but most plants are very forgiving and will usually grow out of pruning mistakes – at worst you may lose some fruit for a season, but pruning mistakes are rarely fatal to a fruit tree.

TOP: **Winter pruning to tidy up a gooseberry cordon.**

MIDDLE: **Cut laterals back to 5cm.**

BOTTOM: **Remove any crossing branches.**

TOP: **Check ties and supports.**

BOTTOM: **Gooseberry after pruning.**

days, to reduce the chance of disease entering the cuts, and when there is no frost. First, decide how you want the tree or bush to grow – this may be a natural tree shape or you may want to grow the tree into a more restricted shape such as a cordon, espalier, fan or something more fancy. In the winter, with the leaves off the tree, the basic structure and outline of the plant can be seen, and any dead, diseased, damaged or crossing and rubbing branches are visible. It is these that should be tackled and removed first, cutting back to healthy tissue/wood. Once this has been done, aim for a simple structure of main branches radiating out from the main trunk. This will give the tree an open look, will help to reduce overcrowding and allow air to circulate. On established trees, leaders – the vigorous new growth from the ends of the main branches – can be cut back by up to a half of the new growth, to an outward-facing bud. Laterals – shoots growing out from around the main branches – can also be trimmed, removing those growing straight up and the wispy 'water shoots' that can congest a tree. Those that are growing more horizontally, in line with the ground, can be left, or shortened back to an upward-facing bud if they are getting too long and straggly.

Note that winter pruning should not be carried out on plums, cherries and other prunus species, as there is a high risk of fungal disease entering the cuts. Pruning plums or cherries for shape can begin once the sap starts rising in the spring, so that as the sap weeps out of the pruning cuts it carries away with it any fungal infection. Leave the pruning of plums and cherries until June, but it should be completed by mid-August, certainly by the end of that month. Any large cuts should be covered immediately with a horticultural wound paint. Winter pruning of grape vines should be completed by the end of December, because after that there is a risk that the pruning cuts will 'bleed' sap and weaken the plant.

Each fruit section contains detailed advice for pruning, but in general there are four basic reasons for pruning.

Pruning for Shape

This is best carried out during the period when the plant is dormant and temperatures are low, usually from November through to February, and so called winter pruning. Winter pruning is best done on dry

Pruning for Tidiness

Linked closely to pruning for shape, pruning for tidiness – to keep the tree within the space allowed – is best done in the winter in the same way as pruning for shape (but do not prune plums in the winter). However, there may be other times of the year when new growth is such that it is starting to get in the way of gardening. If you do need to 'cut back' a tree, just be sensible, try to avoid cutting when the tree is trying to produce fruit, during flowering and fruit set, and only cut what is essential. Removing the odd bit of new growth that is in the way is unlikely to cause too much damage.

Pruning for Vigour

Winter pruning is used to stimulate new, vigorous growth. This is especially useful for producing the

ABOVE: **Redcurrant after winter pruning.**

BELOW: **Winter prune redcurrant laterals to 2.5cm.**

Redcurrant before winter pruning.

Apple cordon before summer pruning.

Summer prune laterals back to an established spur system.

main structural branches on newly planted trees or for producing replacement branches to improve the overall balance and look of a tree. Winter pruning in successive years can be used variously to get a maiden tree to grow and produce branches, to encourage a cordon to grow to its final length, and to stimulate restricted forms such as pyramids or espaliers to produce their next set of branches.

Pruning for Fruit

This is commonly referred to as 'summer pruning' and is usually carried out between mid-June and the end of August, depending on the season and the condition of the fruit tree. Summer pruning is based on cutting back this year's young, vigorous, new growth during the summer months to expose the fruit to sun and fresh air and get the plant into good condition, ready for fruiting next year. Cutting back this year's new growth at the right time will encourage the tree to put its energy into producing fruiting buds for next year rather than into more leafy growth. Most apples and pears, gooseberries and redcurrants produce their flowers and fruit on 'spurs' – short growths from the main branches; summer pruning will encourage the tree to produce more spurs and thus more fruit. Summer pruning also opens up the tree and allows air and sunshine to reach this year's fruit to help it ripen. But what is the 'right time' for summer pruning? Rather than be driven by the calendar to decide on when to prune, keep a close watch on the fruit trees and bushes and it will become clear when summer pruning needs to be done.

Root Pruning

This is done to restrict the vigour of a tree and to stimulate it to produce fruit rather than roots. Some gardeners say that root pruning 'shocks' the tree and its natural reaction is to produce more fruit to help ensure its survival. Root pruning was a common practice in Victorian fruit gardens, as a way of rejuvenating unproductive fruit trees, but it seems to have drifted

Summer pruning new growth to one leaf above the basal cluster.

out of use in recent years. Nevertheless, it can be a helpful technique. On well-established trees, root pruning can be achieved by using a sharp spade to dig a trench around a tree, 1–1.5m or so away from the trunk, severing any roots that are found radiating into the trench. For old or precious trees, just dig round in a semi-circle one season, and dig the remaining half the following season. The soil in the trench can be refreshed with compost or a general-purpose fertilizer, and replaced in the trench. Younger or smaller trees can simply be dug up during the dormant period and replanted immediately. During this process some roots will be damaged and effectively 'pruned'.

A more organized approach is to lift the tree out of the ground and tidy up the root system. Tease out the roots with a fork and inspect the rootball. Remove any damaged or straggly roots, and any that show signs of rot or fungal attack, with a sharp knife or secateurs, plus up to 15 per cent of the thicker anchor-

Make the pruning cut at an angle sloping away from the bud.

age roots around the rootball. Dust the cut ends with yellow sulphur powder to reduce the risk of fungal infection, refresh the soil with a general-purpose fertilizer, then replant. Add support if necessary as some of the anchorage roots will now be missing. It is not generally necessary to root prune soft fruit bushes, but apples, pears, plums and cherries may all be treated this way.

Pruning Technique

Use sharp, good-quality secateurs, a saw or a knife, depending on the thickness of the branch being pruned. Sharp tools are much safer to use as less effort is required to make the cut, so there is less chance of the blade slipping and thus potentially causing injury. Sharp blades will also give a clean cut, leaving no snags or torn bark, which can be an entry point for disease.

Although there may be exceptions, pruning cuts in general should be made just above an upward-pointing, outward-facing bud, the cut being made at an angle across the branch, sloping away from the bud. Making the cut just above the bud will help reduce the chance of die-back which can occur on a stub (a bare length of branch left above a bud); it will also help the new growth get away cleanly, without snagging on any unpruned stubs. Choosing an upward-pointing bud is usually preferable as it will have plenty of vigour and will help keep the new growth up and away from the ground, where the fruit can get dirty or damaged; choosing an outward-facing bud means that the new shoot will grow out from the centre of the tree or bush and reduce the chance of the tree becoming overcrowded or the branches crossing and rubbing. If an outward-facing bud produces new growth that is too upright, it can be brought down closer to the horizontal by tying it down to a stake or peg in the ground, or weighing it down by tying it to something heavy, such as a brick. If it is judged to be in the wrong place, crossing other branches or creating an imbalance, it can be pruned out completely. Making the cut at an angle sloping away from the bud means that any moisture that gathers on the cut end is more likely to drain away from the bud, rather than pooling on the cut end and creating a potential entry point for infection.

When pruning branches over about 20mm (¾in) in diameter, it is safer and easier to use long-handled pruners or loppers. The long handles provide additional leverage, which reduces the chance of damage to your wrists and enables you to exert extra force on the blades. Long-handled pruners will give a clean cut on slightly thicker branches, 20–25mm (¾–1in), with relative ease. For thicker branches, a pruning saw will be needed. When using a pruning saw, it can be helpful to make an initial cut upwards from underneath the branch, before sawing through from the top side; this reduces the chance of the branch falling under its own weight before the saw cut is completely through, which will tear the bark, damage the tree and risk the entry of disease. When sawing very large or heavy branches, even more care needs to be taken. It is often advisable to cut out branches in two stages. First remove the bulk of the branch by making a cut on the waste side, up to 25cm (10in) beyond the final cut. This also reduces the chance of the branch breaking before the cut is completed, and tearing the bark that remains. After the bulk of the branch has been removed, the remainder can be cut more precisely to where the finished cut is required.

Staying safe is an important consideration when sawing branches, and having a second person to support the branch while it is being cut can be very helpful. Another way to make the sawing of large branches safer is to support the length of branch to be removed with a rope lashed to a higher branch or another part of the tree so that it does not crash down when cut, damaging other parts of the tree and creating a danger for anyone standing below. Overall, the best plan for tackling the cutting or removal of large branches may be to carry out a risk assessment, consider the dangers and what could go wrong, and

decide whether it might be more sensible to hire the services of a professional tree surgeon to do the job!

Pruning Tools

Secateurs

These hand-held tools produce a sharp cutting action as the two blades cross each other in a scissors action (so-called 'bypass' secateurs). They give a clean cut and are suitable for branches up to 20mm (¾in) in diameter. If there is a lot of pruning to be done on a regular basis, consider a pair of secateurs with a rotating handle, designed to lessen the strain on the wrist and reduce the chance of repetitive strain injury. Left-handed secateurs are also available that make the job much easier for left-handed gardeners. Some gardeners prefer the traditional 'anvil' secateurs where a single blade cuts down through a branch on to a fixed 'anvil' of softer metal; the risk with this type of secateurs is that the branch will get crushed rather than cut, leading to dieback.

Long-handled Pruners

These are similar to secateurs, but the long handles increase the leverage that can be exerted and thus enable thicker branches to be cut cleanly, up to 25mm (¾in) in diameter. Long-handled pruners, sometimes called 'loppers', also enable the pruning of higher branches without the need for a ladder, although care must be taken not to over-reach. If you are working on overhead branches, it is important to protect yourself from falling leaves and branches; always wear a safety helmet and some form of eye protection, such as safety glasses or a visor.

Saws

Pruning saws have fine, sharp teeth, set in a narrow, usually curved, blade, which can be used in confined spaces between branches without damaging the branches that are to be left uncut. They also work the opposite way to most general saws, as the teeth cut as the blade is drawn back across a branch, rather than cutting when pushed forwards. This reverse action means that cuts can be more precise, and the chance of damage caused by pushing the saw and the branch away is reduced. Fixed to long poles or handles, pruning saws can also be used for cutting branches high in a tree, without the need for a ladder. Again, care must be taken not to over-reach and risk injury, and to protect from falling branches.

Knife

Pruning knives have strong curved blades, which are used with an upward cutting action, pulling up and away from a branch. They are usually of the folding 'penknife' type, although very strong fixed-blade types are available. Like all knives, pruning knives must be kept sharp to make sure that the cut is clean and to reduce the need for using excessive force when cutting, which can lead to slipping and potential injury.

Care of Pruning Tools

Disease can be passed from plant to plant on the blades of pruning tools, so it is important to keep the blades clean as you move from plant to plant. This can be done by wiping the blade between plants with a rubbing alcohol, such as surgical spirit. Alternatively, use an anti-bacterial spray of the type sold for use on kitchen surfaces – spray the blade then wipe it clean

Branches tied down to encourage the development of fruit buds.

for each plant. Keep secateurs out of the dirt by carrying and storing them in a protective holster.

A wipe-over with a light mineral oil will keep pruning tools rust-free and lubricate secateurs and pruners.

Keep knife blades sharp by using a sharpening stone regularly during pruning. Fold blades or fit them into a sheath when not in use to protect the blades and reduce the risk of accidental cuts.

Saw blades should be kept physically clean by brushing and removing any plant debris caught in the saw teeth, to avoid the development of fungal problems. Like secateurs and knives, saws should also be cleaned between use with rubbing alcohol or anti-bacterial spray. It is difficult to sharpen saw blades, beyond making sure that there is still a 'set' on the saw teeth – the 'set' means that the cutting teeth are splayed out slightly from the body of the saw blade, so giving a cut that is slightly wider than the blade itself, so that the saw goes through the wood easily without binding or sticking. Some types of pruning saw have blades that are replaceable, and a new blade is a sure way to make certain that pruning will be carried out safely and effectively.

Blades on secateurs can be sharpened on a stone, but this can be awkward to do. Specially designed secateur sharpeners are available. Alternatively, manufacturers of good-quality secateurs offer a sharpening and refurbishment service. This means that secateurs can be sent away for an annual service when they are not being used, and they return as good as new – clean, sharp and ready for the next season's pruning.

CARE AND PROTECTION

Garden Hygiene

Like any other living organism, fruit trees and bushes are subject to a wide range of pests and diseases. Some, like aphids of one type or another, will affect most plants, while others, such as American gooseberry mildew, will be specific to particular types of fruit. In the wild, where there is a more natural balance between pests and predators, the pests will be controlled to some degree and kept in check, and are less likely to cause too many problems. Specific diseases that affect fruit plants are also less of an issue in the wild because, across a diverse range of plants, no single disease is likely to take hold and cause too much damage. However, in the artificial growing conditions created in a garden, where fruit trees are concentrated into a relatively small area and grown unnaturally close together, problems may build up that can have a dramatic effect on the fruit plants and the crop. Garden fences and close planting, for example, reduce air flow, providing ideal conditions for mildew. A row of one single type of fruit will be very attractive to some pests, as it provides a concentration of foodstuff in a small area, greatly improving the breeding and survival chances of that pest. The use of nets further reduces the opportunity for natural predators, such as blue tits and other small insect-eating birds, to get at the pests that are causing the problem. Because of the unnatural conditions in most gardens, it is vitally important to maintain a high level of garden hygiene, to reduce the opportunity for disease to take hold.

RIGHT: **Pick up fallen leaves in autumn.**

OPPOSITE PAGE: **Soft fruits protected in a fruit cage.**

In practice, there are some very basic steps that will reduce the opportunity for disease to take hold in the garden:

- Always keep knives, secateurs and other cutting tools clean, wiping the blade between plants with a rubbing alcohol, such as surgical spirit. Alternatively, use an anti-bacterial spray of the type sold for use on kitchen surfaces – spray the blade then wipe it clean for each plant. Keep secateurs out of the dirt by carrying and storing them in a protective holster. Disease can be passed from plant to plant on the blades of pruning tools, so it is important to keep the blades clean and sterile.
- Keep mulches away from the base of plants, and try to prevent it touching the plant itself – this will reduce the chance of attacks by soil-borne fungi such as *Phytophthora*.
- Pick up and burn or dispose of any prunings, twigs or woody material that is lying around, as this will remove any potential host for coral spot fungus (*Nectria cinnabarina*).
- Pick up as many leaves from under fruit as possible in the autumn: if they are healthy, turn them

Investigate any fungus.

into leafmould; if they are unhealthy, for example showing signs of scab or leaf spot, do not attempt to compost them but dispose of them by burning or through a local authority composting scheme where the temperatures reached will be high enough to kill the spores.

- Remove any plants or parts of plants that appear to be dead, or are showing signs of disease, by cutting back to healthy tissue; if left, they could start to infect other similar plants nearby and you could lose all of them.
- Investigate any mushrooms, toadstools or fungi that suddenly appear in the vicinity of the fruit – they may be benign, or they may be an indication of a grave problem such as honey fungus.
- Try to replant in fresh areas of the garden where fruit has not been grown for a number of years. This will reduce the chance of soil-borne problems being passed directly from old plants to new plants.

There are also some basic steps that will reduce the number of fruit pests in the garden:

- Deal with leaf-eating larvae, such as gooseberry sawfly, as soon as the problem is first spotted. If left, the pest will quickly strip leaves and weaken the plant; by tackling the first brood early on, subsequent broods will be reduced.
- Use pheromone traps. These are available to control a number of pests such as codling moth, plum

moth and raspberry beetle – most work by using the female pheromone to attract the male insect into a trap, where he either gets stuck or falls into a vessel from which he cannot escape. Pheromone traps were designed to provide an indication of when to spray – the trapped male insects are counted daily, and when the daily count reaches a given point spraying is advised. However, many fruit growers prefer not to spray chemicals on their fruit and use the traps solely to control and eliminate the pest. Pheromone traps for codling moth and plum moth are usually hung in the general area of the fruit trees as the weather starts to warm up, generally from early May, and they need to be in place throughout the summer, renewing the source of the pheromone mid-way. The raspberry beetle trap, which is also effective for controlling this pest on blackberries, loganberries and other hybrid berries, should be hung before the flowers open, so that it is in place when the beetles come looking for the flowers.

Gooseberry sawfly damage.

Pheromone trap hanging in a plum tree.

Encouraging Natural Predators

For every pest there will be a natural predator. This may be an insect-eating bird, such as the blue tit, or it may be another insect, such as a ladybird. Natural predators have a number of advantages over the use of chemicals to control pests – there is no direct cost, there is no chemical residue left on the fruit, and they add a wonderful diversity to the natural life that we see in a garden.

Natural Predators

Birds: garden birds provide an invaluable service to the fruit grower: blackbirds and robins will turn over soil beneath fruit bushes foraging for pests like the pupae of gooseberry sawfly; blue tits and other members of the tit family eat vast quantities of aphids and will help to remove the pest from new shoots in the spring; tits and other insect-eating birds will also do a good job of clearing gooseberry sawfly larvae and other larvae that eat the leaves of fruit trees and bushes, especially

when they have young to feed. Birds can be attracted into the fruit garden in the early spring by hanging bird feeders near the trees and bushes, and keeping shallow bowls of fresh water nearby. The use of nest boxes, designed for robins and tits, will help to make sure that there are lots of hungry young birds to feed with larvae pests. Keeping the net off the roof of the

Ladybirds are voracious natural predators of aphids.

fruit cage until the last minute – until the fruit starts to colour – will mean that the birds will be able to spend the maximum time in and around the fruit bushes. Birds in the right place at the right time can be great friends for fruit growers. However, once the fruit does start to colour, the roof of the fruit cage must be netted, or the larger fruit-eating birds such as blackbirds and thrushes will devour soft fruits such as redcurrants and strawberries. (They seem to prefer red fruits to any other.) Later in the summer it is good policy to net apples and peaches as it will prevent birds from pecking the ripening fruit and providing an entry point for brown rot.

An insect hotel provides homes for lacewings, hoverflies and ladybirds, and is a great way to encourage natural predators into the garden.

Ladybirds are useful inside the fruit cage.

ABOVE: **Blue tits are natural predators that devour aphids and other insect pests.**

LEFT: **Peach with brown rot, having been pecked by a bird.**

Ladybirds, lacewings, hoverflies: these are really beneficial insects to the fruit grower, and encouraging them by providing the perfect habitat for them to live, breed and multiply will help control a wide range of pests. Adult ladybirds will eat aphids, but it is their larvae – looking like tiny black and orange dragons – that have the most voracious appetite for these pests; adult lacewings are strictly honey, pollen and nectar eaters, but their larvae will eat all kinds of pest, including aphids, whiteflies, mealybugs, spider mites, caterpillar eggs and scale insects; like the lacewings, adult hoverflies live on pollen and nectar, but their larvae eat aphids, thrips and other sap-sucking insects.

Wasps: not everyone's favourite insect, often provoking a panic reaction and the desire to destroy, but wasps perform a particularly useful service for fruit growers early in the year. In the spring, when feeding their own larvae, wasps will take whole caterpillars back to their nests. This activity usually coincides with the emergence of the first brood of gooseberry sawfly larvae, which are ideal food for the wasp larvae. It only needs a few wasps to help you keep on top of the gooseberry sawfly problem. Later in the season, when there are no wasp larvae to feed and fruit starts to ripen, wasps can become an annoyance, particularly in and around plum or peach trees. Adult wasps can sense the sweet juice inside and puncture the fruit, providing an entry point for brown rot and leading to the deterioration of the fruit.

Nematodes: these microscopic worms are found in most natural habitats. Their relevance to fruit growing lies in the selection and application of particular nematodes that perform a useful function in getting rid of garden pests. The most widely available and commonly used is probably the vine weevil nematode, which is watered into containers or on to ground that is thought to be infested with vine weevil larvae. The nematodes attack, infest and ultimately kill the larvae. Dispersal in water is the most usual way of spreading and applying nematodes, which, in addition to the treatment of vine weevil, are available for the treatment of slugs, large white butterfly larvae and caterpillars in general, and even codling moth pupae overwintering in the ground beneath apple trees.

Improving Pollination

It is a fact that very few plants will produce worthwhile fruit without their flowers first being pollinated. Pollination is vital for fertilizing the flowers and starting the process that will ultimately lead to the production of fruit, fruit being merely the fleshy container for the seeds which will ensure the perpetuation of the

plant and the start of the next cycle of regeneration and growth. Cross-pollination between two different plants will help to make certain that the gene pool is not weakened by in-breeding and that the strongest genes go on to improve the quality of the species. All of this will, of course, happen in nature without any intervention by mankind, but the fruit grower can help nature and at the same time improve the quality of fruit they are producing.

The most straightforward way to improve pollination is to plant more than one of any particular fruit

A *John Downie* crab apple in flower will pollinate a whole range of apples.

– two different apples, two different pears, etc. – and as long as they are both from the same or adjacent flowering groups, and therefore in flower at the same time, this should help each tree to become pollinated by a different tree. Some fruits are better than others at producing pollen, and in the case of apples it is a good idea to include a flowering crab apple (*Malus*) in any selection of apple trees you make for your garden. Crab apples need not take up much room, and can be grown as single cordon columns; some, like *John Downie*, will produce fruit that is large and suitable for wine-making or crab apple jelly, while others, like *Golden Hornet*, will provide plenty of pollen but only small fruit. Some apples, known as 'triploids', produce little pollen themselves, so even if you grew a second variety only the triploid would be pollinated; in this

situation you will need to grow a third variety of apple to ensure that all the trees get pollinated and bear fruit. In practice, it may be that a tree in a neighbour's garden can provide the pollen, but you can never be certain.

Most fruit trees are pollinated by insects, which means that the weather can affect pollination. Too cold or too wet and the insects will not fly, but there is little that the fruit grower can do to change this. The honey bee is an important insect for pollinating fruit, and the introduction of a hive of honey bees will certainly do a lot to improve pollination, but may not be totally practical in a garden situation. But there are a number of things that the fruit grower can do to encourage more honey bees and other pollinating insects to visit the garden: leave an area

A diversity of flowers in the garden will attract pollinating insects.

of the garden uncultivated to provide a nest site for bumble bees; set up nest boxes comprising closely packed cardboard or cane tubes for solitary bees like the mason bee; grow plants that flower early and are rich in nectar, and these will attract bees, hoverflies and other pollinating insects into the garden. Such plants include crocus, snowdrops, hellebore, winter aconite, the winter-flowering honeysuckle (*Lonicera fragrantissima*) and other similar garden favourites; blackthorn in the hedgerow will also be a valuable early source of nectar for insects.

Finally, if you really want to make sure that pollination occurs, you can always carry out the insects' job yourself, with the aid of a soft, watercolour artist's paintbrush. This can be most effective for peaches, nectarines and apricots which come into flower early in the spring, when the weather may be too cold for pollinating insects to fly. Choose a warm sunny day, when the flowers on the fruit tree are open fully and the pollen is 'ripe' – you will be able to see dusty yellow pollen on the anthers of the flowers. Use the tip of the brush to gently transfer the pollen from the anthers to the stigma of the flower – usually located right in the centre of the flower, glistening and receptive to the pollen. To make sure that pollination is effective, this operation may need to be done on a number of different days, as the flowers open and the pollen ripens.

Thinning

Thinning is the deliberate removal of a proportion of immature fruit from a tree or bush to reduce the total number of fruits that are allowed to ripen to maturity. This is done to reduce the stress on a tree that is over-laden with fruit, to reduce the chance of the tree going into biennial cropping, and to improve the overall size and quality of the fruit that remain after thinning. Thinning can be very stressful for a fruit grower, as it sometimes seems that more of the precious fruit is being removed than is left on the tree. There is an apocryphal story that, in the past, commercial fruit growers asked their neighbours to do the thinning for them, as they were more objective and less sentimental towards the crop. However, research has shown that, although there may be fewer individual fruits left on a tree, the total weight of fruit produced will be the same as for a tree that has not been thinned. This means that the individual fruits will be larger and heavier; conversely, although there may be numerically more individual fruits on a tree that has not been thinned, they will each be smaller.

Fruits that are diseased or infested with maggots can be removed effectively during thinning. In particular, it has been noted that, on plums for example, the first fruits to show signs of ripening are often the ones that contain a plum moth maggot – these are the ones to thin out first.

Thinning does not have to be done all at once. Indeed, it can be beneficial to spread the thinning over a number of weeks, keeping an eye on the natural fruit fall, sometimes called the 'June drop', and reducing the fruit gradually in a number of sweeps. This means that you can keep removing any fruit that gets damaged or diseased subsequently, and as the fruit develops the spacing between the individual fruits can be adjusted.

Although some fruits may come off the tree in your hand as you examine them, thinning is best carried out using secateurs. This will remove the fruit cleanly, without damaging the fruiting spur or tip; as cutting is a deliberate action it also reduces the risk of accidentally knocking off fruit that remain. Try not to nick any fruit that is left with the blade, as this will create an entry point for disease. Do not just pull the fruit off, as this can break or damage the branch.

Heavy cropping plums will benefit from thinning.

Apples: from June, remove any small or underdeveloped fruitlets; remove the 'king fruit' (the central apple of a cluster, which can be identified by the elongated and oblong shape as it develops); and remove fruit that is under a branch and unlikely to receive much sunlight. By July dessert apples should have been thinned to one or two per cluster 10cm (4in) apart, while cookers should be thinned to about 20cm (8in) apart.

A mature 'king fruit' is obvious by the distortion around an overly thick stem.

Apricots: from June, before the fruits are the size of a small walnut, thin to about 10cm (4in) apart.

Blackcurrants: unless grown for exhibition purposes, it is not usual to thin blackcurrants. To do so, remove a proportion of the strigs, focusing on those that are incomplete or contain small, poorly formed fruit, leaving complete strigs to develop fully.

Cane fruit: in general, it is not usually necessary to thin cane fruits such as raspberries, blackberries, etc., as they seem to produce in abundance, but exhibition growers will remove a proportion of the crop to let those that remain grow larger.

Gooseberries: there is a fruit-growing tradition that you thin gooseberries at Whitsun, or the spring bank holiday; the idea is to remove about every other fruit, which will mean that the fruit that is left to ripen will be larger and juicier as a result; the gooseberries that are removed will be green and not yet ripe, but with a little sugar will be perfect for an early pie.

Peaches: from May, once the fruits are the size of a marble, start to thin over a number of weeks as the fruits develop, aiming to end up with fruits spaced about 15–20cm (6–8in) apart. Remove any hanging under branches or leaves and out of the sun. Never allow fruits to develop in pairs, as where they touch they will attract insects that can damage the delicate skin, and any such damage will become a potential site for brown rot to start to develop and ruin the fruit.

Overcrowded immature peaches that need thinning.

Pears: any immature fruitlets that show signs of pear midge, becoming black and distorted, should be removed in May and destroyed – do not compost them. From June, follow the natural fruit drop and remove any small or underdeveloped fruitlets; also remove small fruit, and those hanging hidden beneath a branch and unlikely to receive much sunlight. By July, pears should have been thinned to clusters of one or two fruits, 8-10cm (3–4in) apart.

Plums: there will be an initial drop of small fruit during May. Start to thin as the fruit swells through June, taking off any that show signs of damage or premature

A crowded group of plums: the centre plum could be removed when thinning.

ripening as this is a sure sign that the fruit is infested by the larvae of the plum moth. Do not leave fallen fruit to lie on the ground and rot, but do not compost them. Continue thinning through late June and July, removing any that become damaged or pecked, any with brown rot, and any that are sticky and leaking. For large plums, aim to leave about 7.5–10cm (3–4in) between fruits – this may seem drastic but it will prevent them banging together in the wind and getting bruised; smaller plums could be left slightly closer. Thinning heavy crops of plums reduces the likelihood of the branches breaking under the weight of fruit, and should help to reduce the risk of the tree going into biennial bearing. The overall weight of fruit will be more or less the same, but the fruit that remains will be larger and of better quality than if left unthinned.

Plums after thinning, spaced about a hand's width apart.

Redcurrants and White Currants: unless grown for exhibition purposes, it is not usual to thin these currants, but if it is done, simply remove a proportion of the strigs, focusing on those that are incomplete or poorly formed, leaving complete strigs to develop fully.

Strawberries: most fruit growers want the maximum crop from their strawberries, but exhibition growers will remove a proportion of the crop to let those that remain grow larger. Thinning strawberry runners is a good idea, depending on how many new plants you want to propagate – remove all but one or two runners per plant as they develop. Strawberry beds are sometimes thinned, removing old or diseased plants and excess runners to make room for healthy plants.

Protection from the Weather

Most of the fruit dealt with in this book will be hardy in most places in the British Isles. This means that under 'normal' growing conditions, fruit trees and bushes will not require any artificial protection from the British weather. However, there are exceptions, and there are certain times when it is advantageous to take steps to protect your fruit.

Frost

During the winter months frost is rarely a problem for hardy fruit trees and bushes. In fact, a period of cold chill – where the tree goes into a period of rest and hibernation – is an essential requirement to help replenish its energy ready for the spring. Warm, frost-free winters do not allow sufficient time for the trees to rest and they can become exhausted with the effort of trying to keep growing through a mild winter, resulting in inferior growth and fruiting the next season.

Frost during the flowering period or when the fruit is at an embryo stage is another matter entirely. Frost can destroy the delicate stigma of the flower, preventing fertilization. If there is no fertilization, there will be no fruit. To prevent this happening, the fruit grower must keep a watchful eye on weather forecasts during the flowering period, and protect the flowers if frost is forecast. It is also worth learning the local signs for frost which may not be picked up by regional or more general weather forecasts: a maximum:minimum (Max–Min) thermometer in the garden can be used to record the onset of cold nights, one can feel that the air is frosty, and clear, cloudless nights are a good indicator that frost may be imminent. It is difficult to give frost protection to tall trees or large areas of fruit – commercial growers can achieve this with the use of continuous water spraying and other techniques, but this is not always possible for the amateur fruit grower. In a garden situation, fruit blossom can be protected by covering with a layer of horticultural fleece. Take care to prevent the fleece coming into direct contact with the blossom, as frost forming on the outside of the fleece can still freeze and damage flowers touching the fleece underneath; after all, the

Strawberry plants on a frosty day.

LEFT: **Delicate redcurrant flowers.**

BELOW: **Buds can be damaged by frost.**

fleece is very thin. A double layer of fleece will, of course, double the protection. Old net curtains, old blankets and hessian can also be used to protect flowers from frost, but as these tend to be heavier than horticultural fleece, their weight could damage the flowers if they were to be laid directly on to the plant. This problem can be avoided by constructing a framework of garden canes around the plant and hanging the protection on the frame, or by using the support wires for cordon or cane fruit to take the weight. A fruit cage can be given some protection from frost by hanging old net curtains, blankets or hessian along the east-facing side to protect the blossom from the early morning sun, which will scorch any frozen, but otherwise undamaged, flowers.

Cold, bright, spring days, with cloudless skies leading to a cloudless night, are a good sign that a spring frost could be imminent.

BELOW: Delicate fruit blossom may need protecting from frost or the crop could be lost.

Small embryo fruits are vulnerable to frost damage.

A ready supply of clothes pegs will make the job of covering fruit with horticultural fleece or other materials much easier as they can be attached and removed quickly, and will hold the covers in place.

Frost can also cause damage to small, embryo fruits by freezing them, destroying the delicate cells and causing the fruit to drop off. On larger, more developed fruit, frost can damage the skin cells in areas exposed to the frost, creating a rough or russeted area which will remain on the fruit as it develops.

The choice of site can also influence the extent to which fruit trees are likely to be affected by frost. Remember that as warm air rises, so cold air falls. Avoid planting in 'frost pockets' – low areas of land where the cold air sinks and cannot escape, and provide 'frost gates' – gaps in hedges or fences through which the cold air can drain away. Planting on a slope will also allow the cold air to fall away, but remember that it may gather at the bottom of the slope and form a frost pocket there.

Wind

High winds can cause damage by breaking branches, especially when they are laden with fruit – support heavy branches by tying them to stakes or by maypoling. Wind can also cause unstaked trees to rock; this will make them less stable and more liable to be pulled over when they are covered with heavy fruit; 'wind rock' will also create a gap around the trunk where it enters the ground, which can fill with water and damage the roots. The best protection against the wind is to make sure that fruit trees and bushes are well supported, staked or tied to wires as appropriate; check ties regularly to make sure that they are still in place and have not deteriorated, and also that they have not become too tight so that they damage the bark. Renew and replace stakes and ties as necessary.

Heavy Rain

For fruit trees in areas of poor drainage, excess rain can cause problems by flooding the soil and preventing vital oxygen reaching the roots – in effect, drowning the tree. Wet conditions and waterlogged ground will also encourage problems such as scab. Fruit growers can do little about the total amount of rain that falls, but the soil and planting area can be improved.

Digging the area should help improve drainage, by breaking up any hard 'pan' that may have formed below the surface. Horticultural grit dug into the planting area, and regular top dressing with horticultural grit, should also help. If this approach is not practical, raise up the soil into a ridge above the general level and plant into this. For single trees or bushes the soil could be raised in a mound, into which the fruit is planted.

Lack of Rain

Established fruit trees will tolerate a degree of drought, provided they have got their roots down deep, into damper soil. New plantings will benefit greatly and become established much more quickly if they are watered regularly during the first season after planting. In dry conditions it is best to irrigate well once a week, so that the water can penetrate the soil, rather than a little each day, as this will encourage the roots to come to the surface, where they will dry out more quickly, stressing the plant. This is an even greater problem for fruit such as gooseberries, which naturally tend to have surface roots. Mulching the ground around the fruit will help: use compost, grass mowings, even several layers of newspaper will help if nothing else is available, then water into the mulch and keep it damp. Make sure that the mulch does not come into direct contact with the stem or trunk of the plants as this could become a site for fungal infection.

In dry areas it can be helpful to raise a ridge of soil in a circle around plants to create a saucer-like effect with the plant or tree in the centre. Depending on the size of the plant, this could be 0.5–1m (20–39in) across. The idea is that water applied to the plant will then be concentrated in the area around the plant and not be wasted by running away.

A newly planted tree circled by a ridge of soil to conserve water.

Plums that have burst their skins after a deluge of rain following dry conditions.

The one time when it is essential to protect fruit from rain is when growing peaches or nectarines out of doors. From the end of the year, certainly from January until the end of May, protect peaches and nectarines by covering them with a polythene sheet to prevent the rain touching or splashing on to the emerging buds and leaves. At this time of the year the rain will carry spores of the fungus that causes peach leaf curl (*Taphrina deformans*), a fungal disease which causes the leaves to blister, distort and eventu-

It is essential to keep peaches covered during the winter months to protect against peach leaf curl.

ally drop off. Peach leaf curl looks unsightly and it weakens the tree, with a consequent loss of fruit. It is relatively easy to cover wall-trained peach trees by draping a sheet of polythene over them, fixed to the top of the wall or fence, then supporting and tying it to garden canes across the tree, stopping at about 30cm (12in) up from the ground to allow rain to irrigate the soil in the immediate area of the roots. A sheet of polythene across the peach tree will also help protect the early blossom from frost, and will encourage the fruit to develop earlier. Remember to keep the ends open to allow pollinating insects to reach the blossom. Purpose-built protectors for wall-trained fruit trees can be bought from suppliers of garden equipment.

Hail

Hailstorms often strike without much notice, but if hail is forecast it is worth trying to protect fruit. Tree fruits can be bruised, pitted and damaged when struck by hail, and a build-up of hail lying on fruit as it thaws can cause the surface of the skin to freeze, with resulting damage such as russetting. Horticultural fleece or polythene sheeting will offer some protection from hail.

Sun

While it is certainly true that most fruits need exposure to the sun for ripening, certainly for the development of sugars to make it sweet, there are increasing reports of damage to fruit caused by sunburn from the extremely high temperatures and high levels of ultraviolet light reached by direct exposure to the sun in some areas. The first to suffer have been gooseberries, essentially a woodland plant, where both leaves and fruit have been burned, damaging the plant and rendering the fruit inedible. Apples, too, have been suffering from sunburn in some parts of southern England. If extremely high temperatures are forecast, or are being experienced when the fruit is on the plant, it may help to provide some shade; use sheets of newspaper or horticultural fleece which will diffuse the light.

ABOVE: **Intense sunshine can burn ripe gooseberries.**

BELOW: **Apple showing signs of sunburn.**

Pests, Diseases and Problems

American Gooseberry Mildew

This problem shows itself in two ways: the tips of the new season's growth will show signs of a white powdery mildew, then become stunted and start to die back, and the fruits will develop a white, turning to light brown, velvety coating, which can be peeled off by rubbing the fruits gently. American gooseberry mildew can be managed in a number of ways. For new plantings choose mildew-resistant varieties, such as *Invicta, Greenfinch, Hinnonmaeki Red*, and other new varieties that are being developed. On established plants, pruning to open up the bush and improve the air flow will help reduce the problem as American gooseberry mildew thrives in warm, damp conditions. Summer pruning will effectively remove the tips of laterals and shoots that have been affected, but these should not be put on your compost heap as the fungal spores may not be destroyed if the compost heap does not generate sufficient heat. Instead, burn the affected prunings or dispose of them in a municipal compost collection. Fruits that are affected by American gooseberry mildew may look unappealing but they are still edible: the velvety coating should be rubbed off and the fruit washed before use. Antifungal sprays may have some effect if applied early enough. Follow the manufacturer's instructions, but remember that any fruit that is sprayed must be washed thoroughly before use. Alternatively, spray with a solution of washing soda: 45g dissolved in a litre of warm water, with a little liquid soap solution added to aid 'wetting'.

American gooseberry mildew can also affect blackcurrants that are under stress through drought or nutrient deficiency.

Aphids

Aphids will colonize on soft shoots and young leaves, and if this happens early in the season it can result in complete defoliation as the plant just sheds its damaged leaves. Aphids suck sap from the leaves

The effects of currant blister aphid on a redcurrant leaf.

and excrete a sticky honeydew, which itself can attract mould spores, giving the leaves a sticky/sooty appearance. This will severely weaken the plant and will result in little new growth for next year's fruit and a consequent decline in the crop. Natural predators such as blue tits and the larvae of ladybirds, hoverflies and lacewings will deal effectively with low-level aphid attacks. If the attack is particularly bad, consider washing the leaves with gardener's insecticidal soft soap in a spray, but be aware that this could also affect the natural predators and upset the natural ecological balance on the plants.

Woolly aphids colonize the bark of fruit trees, producing the appearance of small sticky patches of candyfloss. If seen, wipe them off with a cloth dampened with methylated spirits; this will dissolve the sticky protection and expose the aphid itself to drying out or attack from natural predators such as birds.

Apple Sawfly

The larvae of apple sawfly will eat their way across the surface of the fruit, leaving a scar across the skin, before burrowing into the centre of the apple; these fruits will drop before they ripen so that the larvae can pupate and over-winter in the soil. Collect and destroy affected fruit, to break the breeding cycle, but do not compost them.

Bacterial Canker

Bacterial canker affects all *prunus* species, which includes cherries, peaches, nectarines and plums. It shows itself as sunken areas of damage to the bark, which start to ooze a sticky bacterial gum or slime around the edges; affected shoots and branches start to die back, and the leaves may develop small brown spots, which drop out, leaving the classic 'shot hole' appearance. Keeping the tree growing healthily and reducing the stress caused by drought will help to ward off the problem, and some trees may survive for years with these signs, still producing fruit, but bacterial canker will progressively weaken and ultimately kill the tree, or it may become so unsightly that it has to be removed. Cankered branches can be removed during the summer months, cutting back to healthy tissue and painting the cut end with a horticultural wound paint. Burn affected prunings and sterilize pruning tools after use so that the infection is not passed from tree to tree. If it is feasible to spray the tree, copper-based fungicides such as Bordeaux Mixture can be effective against bacterial canker; apply as recommended by the manufacturer, probably three times after the fruit has been picked, from mid-summer into early autumn. Plums *Marjorie's Seedling* and *Warwickshire Drooper* are reputed to have some resistance to bacterial canker.

Biennial Bearing

Biennial bearing is a problem that can affect apples, pears and plums, and it happens when a fruit tree gets into a cycle of producing a particularly heavy crop in one year, followed by few if any fruit the next year. The problem can be avoided to some degree by thinning the fruit heavily to reduce the number of fruit that the tree tries to produce each year, and in this way the tree will not be exhausted by the effort and take a year off fruiting to recover. Fruit thinning is good practice as the fruit that remain on the tree will be larger and better quality.

Big Bud Mite

Perhaps more properly known as the blackcurrant gall mite, it lays its eggs in the buds, where they feed and breed. The mites will destroy the bud and stop it developing; they also transmit the dreaded reversion disease If buds seem to be unusually large and round, remove the entire bud by hand and destroy it by crushing or burning.

Birds and Beasts

Most ripe fruits will be attractive to some birds, but in general the darker fruits such as blackberries do not seem to attract birds to the same degree as, say, redcurrants and cherries. More than most ripe fruit, redcurrants and cherries are attractive to birds, especially blackbirds and thrushes, as soon as they start turning pink. Growing soft fruit in a fruit cage stops the problem, and even a net will keep the birds off and give the grower some peace of mind. Apples and pears may also be attractive to birds, especially during dry spells when small birds will peck the top of the fruit for the juice; pecked fruit can be unappetizing and unhealthy, and any damage will provide an entry point for brown rot, which will quickly take over the whole fruit. Growing fruit trees in a fruit cage is not necessarily practical, but small trees can be protected to some degree by throwing a net over the top. Large birds, such as wood pigeons, can also do considerable physical damage by landing in a fruit bush. Netting will help, but a large pigeon will weigh down loose netting and may still cause damage to the top of the bush. Pigeons and magpies will break off new shoots. CDs suspended from wires will rotate and create moving light patterns which disturb birds, and plastic bags pegged to the wires will flap in the wind and have a similar effect, but cherries are a real favourite of birds and they will show a relentless interest in the fruit all the while it hangs on the tree. Failing that, be willing to share the fruit with the birds and take pleasure in the wildlife that your tree and fruit is attracting. Remember to remove bird scaring devices from the tree once the fruit is picked as birds do a great serv-

Hungry birds can damage fruit in different ways.

ice as natural predators, removing aphids and other unwanted insects from the tree.

Foxes and badgers will eat ripe fruit. While a fruit cage will afford some protection, it cannot be guaranteed.

Bitter Pit

Not a pest or disease, but a disorder that can affect apples that have a deficiency of calcium and/or an excess of potassium or magnesium – so how can you tell? Bitter pit shows itself as small sunken areas on the apple skin, and there will be brown, corky deposits beneath the skin and through the fruit. The problem is exacerbated if the tree has been overfed with nitrogen-rich fertilizers, if there are extreme fluctuations

in temperature when the tree is in fruit, and if watering is irregular during periods of drought. Fruit that is picked before it is mature can also develop the signs

Newton Wonder **showing signs of bitter pit on the skin.**

Once cut, diagnosis of bitter pit can be confirmed by the brown cork-like deposits beneath the skin.

by brown rot will dry and shrivel in the branches, taking on a mummified appearance – these should be removed when they are seen as they will infect the whole tree with spores. Spores also overwinter in cankers on damaged shoots. Brown rot also affects fruiting spurs, causing them to shrivel and die, and it will cause blossom wilt. Brown rot is particularly prevalent if it is wet during the flowering period, and if conditions turn warm and humid when the fruit becomes ripe.

of bitter pit during storage. Some varieties seem to be particularly susceptible, including *Bramley's Seedling*, *Edward VII*, *Newton Wonder* and others. Although calcium sprays can help commercial growers, in a garden setting the solution is to improve the way the trees are managed: do not overfeed, try to maintain a balanced supply of water, and use a mulch so that the soil does not dry out completely. Summer pruning is also known to help as it affects how the tree utilizes its supply of calcium, to the benefit of fruiting buds.

An apple badly affected by brown rot.

Botrytis

See Grey mould.

Brown Rot

Brown rot is a common fungal disease that can affect most fruit, but it is particularly evident on tree fruit such as apples, apricots, peaches, pears and plums. Caused by the fungi *Monilinia laxa* and *Monilinia fructigena*, brown rot starts with a small brown spot which develops quickly to cover the entire fruit with concentric rings of spores; the fruit rot throughout and fall to the ground, where they can reinfect the tree as the spores are splashed up by rain; some fruits affected

Plums *Czar*, *Jefferson*, *Ontario* and *President* are said to have some resistance to brown rot, but this cannot be guaranteed under all growing conditions.

The best solution is to maintain a high level of garden hygiene: remove all fruit that shows signs of brown rot, pick up and dispose of all fallen fruit and dead twigs that fall from the tree, and remove spurs that have died, cutting back to healthy wood. Fruit that is pecked or damaged by birds or insects will quickly succumb to brown rot, so protect fruit with nets if feasible. There is no fungicidal spray for brown rot, but keeping the tree healthy will help to build up some resistance.

Canker

Apple and pear canker, *Nectria galligena*, is a fungal problem that shows itself as cracking and discoloured sunken patches on the bark; these sunken areas gradually become lesions of dead and crumbly tissue. If a canker is allowed to develop until it encircles the branch, the whole branch will die. Cut out cankers or remove affected twigs and branches, cutting back to healthy wood; protect exposed cut surfaces with a horticultural wound paint, and sterilize the knife or secateurs to prevent the infection being passed to other trees. The incidence of canker can be reduced by improving the growing conditions, particularly drainage. In areas prone to canker grow apple varieties that have some resistance, such as *Alfriston, Annie Elizabeth, Grenadier, Katy, Newton Wonder*, and others; avoid growing varieties which are particularly susceptible, such as *Cox's Orange Pippin, James Grieve, Worcester Pearmain*, and others.

Codling Moth

This is the major problem for apple growers, and is the traditional maggot that can make an apple rotten to the core. The problem is spotted as a neat hole in the apple skin, and white larvae in the core. This pest can be dealt with effectively by hanging a pheromone trap near the apple trees from early May – the pheromone attracts the male moths, which get trapped on a sticky card across the floor of the trap. The sticky card is disposed of at the end of the season. Depending on the size of the area to be protected, more than one pheromone trap may be required, and the traps may need the pheromone replacing during a particularly bad season.

Coral Spot

This distinctive fungus appears as bright orange,

An extreme example of apple canker.

A pheromone trap is an effective way to deal with the problem of codling moth.

pinhead-sized spots on dead wood, such as a branch that has died back, or on prunings that have been left on the ground beneath the plant. If left, it can cause whole branches to die back. Effective garden hygiene, clearing twigs and prunings from the ground, will help avoid the problem. Affected areas of branches should be removed, cutting back to healthy wood. Do not compost wood that is affected by coral spot; instead burn it or dispose of it in a municipal compost collection.

Currant Clearwing Moth

The larva of this tiny moth burrows its way through the central pith inside the branches of redcurrants. The problem manifests itself when entire branches die back, and the diagnosis is confirmed by inspecting the dead branches; when cut out and removed, they will show a hole through the centre of the branch. Holes may also be discovered at the base of fruit spurs, where the adult moth escapes, having pupated within the branch. There is little that the fruit grower can do to prevent or treat this problem, other than create an environment that supports natural predators such as spiders and harvestmen.

Die-back on Gooseberries and Redcurrants

Entire branches, sometimes whole cordons, will drop the leaves, their buds will fail to develop and the fruits shrivel and fall off. There are many causes of this on gooseberries and redcurrants, such as the larvae of currant clearwing moth, drought or even being tied too tightly to a cane. It is sometimes linked with a particularly bad attack of American gooseberry mildew

Signs of currant clearwing moth damage. The larva has bored through the centre of a redcurrant branch, causing die-back of that branch.

Drought

Lack of water will stop fruits swelling and they will tend to stay dry and seedy. Soft fruits such as black-currants, gooseberries and redcurrants will develop tough skins, which can burst at the first heavy rain. During periods of drought, stressed fruit trees and bushes will drop their fruit and sometimes also their leaves. Reduce the problem by mulching early in the season and watering if necessary.

Recent research suggests that partial root drying need not be a total disaster for strawberries, as it tends to improve the flavour of the crop, as long as sufficient water is available for the fruit to swell.

Frost

Frost will destroy the flowers on fruit trees and bushes, which means that no fruit will be produced by any flowers that are frosted. If frost is forecast when the fruit is in flower, protect the plant by covering it with horticultural fleece or newspaper overnight and during frosty days; fasten the covering down with pegs if conditions are windy. Horticultural fleece can be pegged across trained fruit to protect the side facing the early morning sun, as this can burn and damage flowers that are frozen. Remove the horticultural fleece once the temperature rises to allow any pollinating insects to do their job. Growing early flowering fruit such as apricots, cherries, peaches and nectarines against a wall or fence will help protect the flowers from frost.

Fungal Diseases of Cane Fruit

Cane blight is a fungal infection that attacks cane fruits at ground level. It will first be evident when the leaves on the fruiting canes start to shrivel and die back. Closer inspection will reveal dark patches on these canes at ground level; they will turn brittle and crack, and may show tiny black spores. Cut out affected canes at ground level or remove affected plants. Burn or dispose of affected canes; do not compost them.

The right side of this redcurrant cordon has died back, but the left side remains healthy.

or Botrytis. Remove affected branches by cutting back to healthy wood, and improve the general growing conditions, making sure that the plant gets sufficient water and nutrients to encourage new, healthy growth. Burn or dispose of any wood that is removed.

Spur blight on loganberry.

Do not replant in the same area as the ground will be infected with the fungal spores. Clean and disinfect secateurs used to cut plants with cane spot to prevent cross-infection with healthy plants.

Cane spot attacks cane fruit in May and June, and is a fungal infection that shows itself as small purple spots that grow and start to cause cankers on the cane, or white indentations with a purple edge. Affected canes will tend to die back, and any fruit will be small or distorted. Once affected, there is little that can be done with the cane, so cut it back to ground level in the autumn. Burn or dispose of affected canes; do not compost them. Clean and disinfect secateurs used to cut plants with cane spot to prevent cross-infection with healthy plants.

Purple blotch – as the name suggests, this fungal problem shows itself as purple blotches on new shoots and the lower end of the canes; the main symptom will be the die-back of the entire cane, which means that no fruit will be produced on infected canes. Burn or dispose of affected canes; do not compost them. Clean and disinfect secateurs to prevent cross-infection with healthy plants.

Spur blight causes new canes to develop purple blotches around the leaf buds in August; these blotches change through brown and black to silvery-white over the winter. If these blotches encircle the cane it will not develop, but will start to die back, remaining weak and spindly; buds will fail to develop, failing to produce flowers or fruit. If seen, affected canes should be cut out and burned. As with many garden problems, it is better to avoid spur blight than try to treat it – in the spring thin out weak canes to avoid overcrowding, and do not overuse fertilizers that are high in nitrogen, such as poultry manure, as this will promote soft growth that is more susceptible to spur blight. Sterilize secateurs after cutting canes with spur blight to avoid cross-infection to healthy plants.

Fungal problems in cane fruit can be managed to some degree by growing resistant varieties, thinning canes to reduce overcrowding, keeping a good air flow around plants, and maintaining watering so that plants are not growing under stress. If all these measures fail, a copper-based fungicide applied to the new growth as it emerges from the soil may have a short-term effect on these fungal diseases. If the fungal problems cannot be successfully managed, the best course of action is to remove affected plants. They should be dug up and burned; do not compost them. Start again with new, healthy plants in another part of the garden where the soil is clean and not likely to be infected with the fungal spores. Regular replacement of old plants with new healthy ones will help to reduce fungal problems. Clean and disinfect secateurs used to cut plants with fungal disease to prevent cross-infection with healthy plants.

Gooseberry Sawfly

Gooseberry sawfly is a particular pest of gooseberries, redcurrants and white currants. Often the first sign of an attack by gooseberry sawfly is a branch of skeletal leaves, with no sign of the pest. The adult sawfly lays its eggs deep in the centre of the bush, on the underside of leaves. The larvae hatch at first light and start immediately to eat the leaf. At this stage they are under 1cm long, and resemble pale green threads. As they eat around the edge of the leaf, the larvae get bigger, longer and fatter, developing characteristic black spots along their sides. At the end of the day, if left undisturbed, the satiated larvae drop to the ground where they pupate, emerging a week or so later as adult flies to start the cycle again. Gooseberry sawflies can produce up to three generations each year, starting in late April/early May, and continuing through the summer months to August and September. The effect of gooseberry sawfly larvae on a gooseberry bush can be quite devastating. Starting low down in the centre of the bush, the larvae will eat their way upwards and outwards, defoliating entire branches and the entire bush if not controlled. The effect on the fruit grower can be equally devastating – an apparently healthy bush can be reduced to bare sticks within a day. Such defoliation will weaken the plant and reduce the crop the following year. Vigilance is the best way to deal with gooseberry sawfly. Keep a look out for signs of damage from the end of April. As soon as larvae are seen, remove them from the plant by hand and dispose of them. The larvae seem to start feeding around the edge of the leaf, so the first sign may be an unnaturally straight side to a leaf, where it is being eaten. Tapping the branch can often cause the larvae to arch up and become more visible and thus easier to see and remove. Checking the plant several times a day, starting early in the morning, can be an effective way of controlling the pest – remembering that the larvae will be eating from dawn to dusk, stopping only when they reach a mature size. If the first brood of the season is dealt with thoroughly, subsequent broods will be less of a problem. Spacious planting, leaving plenty of room around the bushes, and pruning the plants to encourage a good air flow will make the gooseberry plants less attractive to the adult sawflies as they dislike being buffeted by the wind, preferring the calm conditions found in an overcrowded bush. It is reported that growing the strong-smelling herb feverfew (*Tanacetum parthenium*) around gooseberries will discourage the adult fly. Natural predators can also be a great help when dealing with gooseberry sawfly: these include blue tits and, perhaps surprisingly, wasps, which will take the live caterpillars to feed their own young. Nematodes are available as a natural control. There are chemical sprays, but be sure to read the instructions carefully before use.

Grey Mould

Grey mould, *Botrytis cinerea*, can develop on the ripe fruit of blackberries, raspberries and other hybrid

The voracious gooseberry sawfly larva.

berries, especially in warm, damp conditions when there is little air circulating. Over-ripe and late in the season fruit will be particularly susceptible. There is no chemical treatment for the amateur fruit grower, so the emphasis should be on prevention rather than cure – keep the plants open and airy, and practise good garden hygiene by removing any mouldy or damaged fruits before the problem can get established.

Honey Fungus

This soil-borne fungus can attack fruit trees and bushes as well as other plants that have bark. Plants that are stressed through drought or another disease will be particularly vulnerable. Symptoms include the sudden death of the plant, or a failure to come into leaf in the spring. Check under the bark at soil level for the characteristic white sheath of fungus; if present, dig up the affected plant and burn it. Remove as much of the old root system from the soil as possible. Make sure that surrounding plants are kept in healthy growth,

as honey fungus will attack plants that are stressed or in poor health. Do not replant the area with anything that has bark, as this could be attacked by spores or rhizomorphs, a root-like part of the fungus, lurking in the soil, but herbaceous plants (with the exception of rhubarb) will be safe.

Fruiting bodies of honey fungus – a bad sign for the fruit grower if it appears on a favourite tree.

Peach Leaf Curl

A serious problem for peaches and nectarines, this disease, caused by spores of the fungus *Taphrina deformans*, will cause the emerging leaves to blister, distort and eventually drop off. In addition to looking unsightly and weakening the tree, it also reduces the cropping potential. The spores are in the air and are carried on to the tree by rain. Protection needs to be in the form of a covering that will prevent rain reaching the branches, buds and leaves on the tree from December until June, while allowing rainwater to reach the roots. This can be achieved more easily when the tree is growing against a wall or fence, as the whole of the back of the tree will be protected, and a polythene cover over the front of the fan will complete the protection. Such covers are available from commercial suppliers, or they can be constructed from a framework of timber or garden canes. The key thing is to keep the rain off the branches, shoots and leaves.

Avalon Pride is marketed as being 'almost completely' resistant to peach leaf curl, and some resistance to the problem is claimed for varieties with 'Red' in the name, such as *Redwing*, but this cannot be guaranteed, as the general health of the trees will vary, as will the growing and weather conditions. As a rule, assume that you will need to cover and protect your peach from peach leaf curl, rather than leave it uncovered and find that it has been affected.

Pear Leaf Blister Mite

This problem is noticed when the leaves develop pink or brown blisters and the edges of the leaves start to turn black and eventually fall prematurely. There is no chemical control for this pest and, although it makes the tree unsightly, it will not damage the fruit. If just a few leaves are affected, remove and destroy them, but this is not practical if the infestation is too extensive, in which case just leave them and make sure that the tree is fed and watered well to help offset any weakness caused by defoliation. Clear away and burn fallen leaves.

Pear Midge

Fruits affected by pear midge will start to grow faster than unaffected fruits; they will take on a more rounded appearance, turn black and eventually fall off. When examined, affected fruits will be filled with small white larvae. This pest will overwinter in the ground as pupae, from which the adult will emerge the following year to repeat the infestation. Pick off any blackened fruit before they fall and destroy the larvae to break the lifecycle; cover the ground beneath pear trees with a polythene sheet to catch the fallen fruit, making it easier to collect and destroy, thus preventing the larvae pupating in the soil. Loosen the soil around pear trees to encourage natural predators, especially birds, to forage for and eat the pupae.

Pear Rust

Easily spotted as bright orange patches on the leaves, which eventually develop horn-shaped points under the leaves, from where this fungal infection discharges its spores. Although it may make the tree look unsightly, it is rarely serious enough to affect the crop. A fungicide is available that claims to control the problem, but if just a few leaves are affected, simply remove and destroy them to reduce the spores that

Distinctive orange patches on the leaf of a pear are often the first sign of pear rust, before the horn-like fruiting bodies of this fungus develop on the underside of the leaves.

are released. This is not practical if the problem is too extensive, in which case just leave them and make sure that the tree is fed and watered well to keep it healthy. Branches may be affected, causing cankers to appear; these should be pruned out and burned. Clear away and burn fallen leaves, but do not compost them. The fungus that causes pear rust, *Gymnosporangium sabinae*, needs to overwinter on a host plant which is juniper, so check any nearby junipers and prune out any sign of the orange rust. Again, burn the prunings, do not compost them.

Phytophthora

This is a soil-borne disease which attacks the plant at ground level, resulting in root rot and the ultimate death of the plant. Keep plants growing healthily and do not allow compost, mulch or other rotting matter to come into direct contact with the plant at soil level.

Plum Moth

This pest is very visible as a lively red larva, wriggling in the centre of a ripe plum. In fact, the fruit is likely to show symptoms of plum moth problems from the outside before the fruit is opened – affected fruit will be the first to ripen, and may start to drop prematurely; they are likely to be sticky, and may ooze a clear gum. As these symptoms occur early, these will be the fruit to remove first, as part of the thinning process – do not compost fruit that has plum moth larvae, as they will pupate over the winter and emerge the following year to renew the attack. The plum moth problem can be dealt with relatively effectively by hanging pheromone traps near the plum trees from early May – the pheromone attracts the male moths, which get trapped on a sticky card across the floor of the trap. The sticky card is disposed of at the end of the season. Depending on the size of the area to be protected, more than one pheromone trap may be required, and the traps may need the pheromone replacing during a particularly bad season.

Potash Deficiency in Gooseberries and Redcurrants

This is evidenced by a reddish tinge to the edges of the leaves, and will result in poor growth and early leaf drop, weakening the plant and reducing the crop in future years. This problem can be addressed with an application of sulphate of potash around the roots in February, and the use of a high potash tomato fertilizer once the fruit has set.

Red colouring on the leaves of soft fruit, like this redcurrant leaf, can indicate a potash deficiency.

Powdery Mildew

Powdery mildew can affect strawberry plants that are overcrowded, creating permanently damp conditions, with poor air flow. It forms as a distinctive white mildew under the leaves and around buds, sometimes showing as purple areas on the top surfaces of leaves. There is no chemical control, but the problem can be avoided by reducing overcrowding, maintaining a good air flow and good garden hygiene. With strawberries, remove old leaves from plants and the ground at the end of the season, and burn them; grow mildew-resistant varieties such as *Cambridge Late Pine, Rhapsody* and others.

On apples and pears powdery mildew appears as a powdery white/grey coating on new shoots, which become distorted and die back. It is often a sign of dryness at the roots, and is more prevalent in dry seasons. Healthy trees are less at risk, and will often grow out of the problem as their vigour increases through the spring. Keep the trees well watered, and remove and destroy badly damaged shoots, but do not compost them. There are fungicides available to help control the problem, but read the manufacturer's instructions carefully before use to make sure that the treatment is suitable for food crops. Some varieties of apple, such as *Cox's Orange Pippin*, are more susceptible to powdery mildew than others, and so more resistant varieties, such as *Alkmene, Discovery, James Grieve, Worcester Pearmain* and others, could be chosen for growing in dry areas.

Cherries, nectarines, peaches and plums are also susceptible to powdery mildew, especially in dry seasons.

Raspberry Beetle

This small brown beetle lays its eggs in the opening flowers from May through to mid-July. The larvae that emerge start to eat the drupelets of the fruit, leaving them dry and seedy at the stalk end. The larvae also eat into the central plug in the fruit, and are often first spotted trying to escape when the fruit is picked. Once they have reached maturity, the larvae drop to the soil below, where they overwinter as pupae, to emerge as beetles the following spring. Chemical controls are available, but although these sprays are applied to the immature fruit, there are still likely to be open flowers, and there is a high risk of killing bees and other pollinating insects. A better solution is to hang a raspberry beetle trap in or near the plants. This will attract the adult beetles and consign them

Young apple shoots showing signs of powdery mildew damage.

to a watery grave within the trap. If picked fruit is left on a white plate before being eaten, the raspberry beetle larvae will tend to drop from the fruit on to the plate, where they can be hand selected for disposal. Fruit that ripens towards the end of the season does not seem to be affected as badly as the earliest fruit, so one approach to control is to remove and dispose of early fruit that is likely to be affected by the beetle larvae, and wait for the later fruit to develop, which will be relatively pest-free.

Loganberries affected by raspberry beetle, showing damage to the drupelets.

Reversion

This is a disease that will stunt the growth and development of blackcurrants, weakening the plant. It is a difficult problem to diagnose, but a decline in the crop is a good clue. Reversion can also be identified by comparing the shape and size of the leaves on a suspect bush with the leaves on a healthy bush. The healthy leaves will be large and green, and the shape of a healthy leaf is more or less the same on both sides of the central stalk, with well spaced ribs and clearly defined points. A leaf from a plant suffering from reversion will be elongated and will show unequal growth on either side of the stalk, giving it a lopsided appearance and rounded points. But one leaf is not sufficient for a confident diagnosis, and confirmation from a recognized gardening organization may be required. However, if there is a suspicion of reversion,

and the plant is unproductive, it may be wiser to dig it out and burn it, replanting another blackcurrant elsewhere in the garden.

Scab

Apple scab, caused by the fungus *Venturia inaequalis*, is a serious problem for apple growers, particularly in cool, wet seasons. It shows itself as a series of dull brown or black 'scabs' on the surface of the fruit, making it look most unappetizing, although, in fact, the fruit can be used once peeled. There are two ways to tackle the problem of scab.

Apple scab on a *Bramley's Seedling*.

The first is garden hygiene. The spores of apple scab overwinter on fallen leaves, twigs and affected fruit, then the spores are splashed back up on to the newly emerging leaves in the spring and the cycle continues and affects the fruit again. Good garden hygiene means picking up and removing all fallen leaves, twigs and fruit in the autumn and disposing of or burning them – do not compost them.

The second approach is to avoid growing varieties that are susceptible to scab, such as the *John Downie* crab apple, *Bramley's Seedling*, *Cox's Orange Pippin*, *James Grieve*, *Laxton's Superb*, *Gala* and others, and instead grow varieties that are reputed to have some resistance to scab, such as *Kidd's Orange Red*,

Limelight, Winter Gem, Lord Derby, Sunset and others. Remember, resistance to scab is not total, and in a 'bad scab year', or in cold, wet areas, most varieties have the potential to have problems with scab.

Pear scab, caused by the fungus *Venturia pirina*, is a serious problem for pear growers, particularly in cool, wet seasons. It shows itself as a series of dull brown or black 'scabs' on the surface of the fruit, making it look most unappetizing, although, in fact, the fruit can be used once peeled. There are two ways to tackle the problem of pear scab.

The first is garden hygiene. The spores of pear scab overwinter on fallen leaves, twigs and affected fruit, then the spores are splashed back up on to the newly emerging leaves in the spring and the cycle continues and affects the fruit again. Good garden hygiene means picking up and removing all fallen leaves, twigs and fruit in the autumn and disposing of or burning them – do not compost them.

The second approach is to avoid growing varieties that are susceptible to scab, such as *Williams' Bon Chrétien*, and instead grow varieties that are reputed to have some resistance to scab, such as *Bristol Cross, Buerré Hardy, Catillac* and others.

Silver Leaf

Silver leaf is a serious disease of apricots, cherries, nectarines, peaches, plums and other *prunus*; it causes die-back of first shoots and then branches; if not dealt with, it will eventually destroy the entire tree. The disease is caused by the fungus *Chondrostereum purpureum*, and is so-called because of the silvery sheen that develops on the leaves of affected shoots and branches. The name of the fungus also gives a clue to a way of identifying the disease, as affected branches that are cut will show a characteristic purple stain within the wood. Severely affected trees will develop characteristic bracket fungus growths, which release spores into the air. These spores enter other trees through wounds or cuts. Affected branches should be cut out, back to healthy wood, and the cut ends protected by painting with a horticultural wound paint. The fungal spores are in the air through-

out most of the year, and enter the tree through wounds, such as pruning cuts. For this reason, cherries and all *prunus* species should not be pruned or cut back during the winter months. Pruning should only be carried out from June, when the sap starts to rise in the trees and will tend to push out any fungal spores which are around, and should be completed by mid-August, or at the latest by the end of that month; as a precaution it is also worth painting any large cuts with a horticultural wound paint to further reduce the chance of silver leaf infection. Generally, keeping trees growing healthily will help to protect them from fungal attack; one of the most effective ways is to reduce the stress caused by drought. Maintain a good standard of garden hygiene, burn all affected timber and sterilize tools and equipment used for cutting and pruning before using on other trees.

'False silver leaf', which is more common than true silver leaf, is a problem caused by lack of nutrients and can be corrected by watering, mulching and feeding the tree with a general purpose fertilizer. For diagnosis purposes, the main differences from true silver leaf are that the whole of the tree will appear to be affected, not just odd branches; there will be little or no die-back of shoots; and cut branches will not show the characteristic purple stain.

Slug and Snails

Slugs and snails can do a lot of damage to fruit on the ground. Strawberry plants grown in the ground are especially vulnerable, with slugs attacking the ripe fruit. Supporting the fruiting truss with straw is the traditional solution, the theory being that slugs and snails do not like moving over the rough straw, but this cannot be guaranteed to be 100 per cent effective. There are chemical controls that can be used against slugs and snails, but for many growers these raise concerns over the potential effect on other wildlife that may eat the poisoned slugs, and the use of such chemicals around fruit that is to be eaten is a worry. Alternatively, there are some non-chemical ways that strawberries can be protected to some degree from slugs and snails: physical barriers –

surround the plants or rows of plants with something that slugs and snails find difficult to cross, such as horticultural grit or sand, crushed eggshells, or used coffee grounds; traps – sink an empty jar or tin in the ground near the strawberries, and half fill it with beer, as this will attract the slugs away from the fruit and into the beer, where they can be disposed of. Another way of trapping slugs is to leave the peel from half a grapefruit nearby; slugs will crawl under it during the day, and can subsequently be removed.

Even strawberries growing in bags or containers are not totally safe as slugs and snails will travel into bags or containers in wet weather, hiding during daylight hours and coming out to feed in the dark. This brings us to the ultimate solution for any situation: hand selection. Inspect each plant carefully each night with a torch, and remove and dispose of any slugs or snails that are discovered.

Verticillium Wilt

This is a fungal disease of strawberries which can build up in the soil. Plants will start to lose their colour, flop and not respond to watering. Eventually the plant will become brown and die. There is no cure as such, the only solution is to dispose of affected plants, roots and soil in the immediate area, and not replant strawberries in the same site. New, healthy plants and fresh uncontaminated soil or compost will help to avoid this problem, and avoid planting on sites which have previously grown chrysanthemums, potatoes or tomatoes.

Strawberry suffering from verticillium wilt.

Vine Weevil

Vine weevil grubs can be a problem for container-grown fruit, eating the roots and weakening the plant. Watch the plant for a lack of new growth and an over-all weakness; check the compost to see if there are any of the white grubs in the rootball. Destroy any grubs that can be seen, by hand. Use a biological control such as a vine weevil nematode to treat containers that are suspected of harbouring vine weevil. Do not reuse the compost as it is likely to spread the problem elsewhere in the garden.

Virus Disease

All cane fruit and strawberries are susceptible to virus diseases, transmitted from plant to plant by aphids and/or tiny eelworms in the soil. Affected plants will continue to produce fruit, but the crop will reduce over time and the quality will decline to hard, under-developed fruit as the plant is gradually weakened. Affected plants will look unhealthy, with yellowing leaves through the growing season – this should not be confused with the natural yellowing and leaf fall which occurs in the autumn. Virus diseases can be held at bay by starting off with plants from reputable growers or nurseries, which are certified as virus-free. For strawberries, build up a rotation system, replacing old plants with new, healthy stock, so that none is older than three or four years. Resist the temptation to accept gifts of canes, suckers or runners from other gardeners, as there is a risk that you may be given plants that are already infected with a virus. If a plant appears to be suffering from virus disease, remove and dispose of the plant, but do not compost it. Replant new stock in a different part of the garden.

Wasps

Wasps can become a problem once fruit becomes ripe, as they will pierce the skin of the fruit for sugar, which encourages brown rot to develop. Wasps can also pose a problem for pickers, as they will be flying around the ripe fruit and threatening to sting. Wasps will also lurk inside fruit, in holes under the skin, where they can sting the unwary as the fruit is being picked. Jam-jar traps hung around the trees will attract, trap and possibly reduce the number flying around, but the best approach is to avoid picking when it is hot and sunny, as the wasps will then be at their most active. Instead, pick in the early morning or evening, or when it is cooler, and just be careful.

Winter Moth and Tortrix Moth Caterpillars

These caterpillars will eat the new leaves as they emerge in the spring. The problem can be control-led by a grease-band around the trunk of the tree from October until the next spring; this will trap the wingless female moths as they climb the tree in the autumn. The grease used must be vegetable-based and designed for this use, so as not to harm the tree. Traditional grease-bands were made of a coated paper that was tied round the trunk, about 45cm (18in) above the ground; this was removed and destroyed in the spring. A more modern way of applying the grease is to extrude a bead of grease around the tree trunk from a cartridge, using a frame-gun.

GROWING FRUIT

Soft Fruits

Blackberry (*Rubus fruticosus*) and Hybrid Berries

The modern blackberry varieties available from garden centres and nurseries, with their evocative names, are all refined descendants of the humble bramble that grows wild in woods, hedgerows and on disused land throughout the country. This ability to grow anywhere demonstrates that, as a plant, it will be relatively easy to grow in the garden, and will not be too fussy about soil type or aspect. Indeed, the main problem with blackberries is containing their exuberant growth and channelling this energy into maximizing fruit production. However, there is one major difference between the brambles growing wild and the varieties available to the gardener, and that is in the consistency of the size and quality of the fruit. We may all have come across a wild bramble that has decent-sized fruit, but for every one like that there will be thousands of wild plants that produce little more than small hard fruit. Sure, wild brambles have a distinctively 'woody' taste that is difficult to replicate in the garden, but modern varieties more than make up for this with their rich flavours and large juicy fruits.

Hybrid berries are fruits that have been developed through crossing various *rubus* species (including blackberry, raspberry, dewberry and others) in different combinations to produce fruits such as the loganberry, tayberry, boysenberry, kings acre berry, and others. All these hybrid berries grow, and are culti-

vated, in a similar way to the blackberry, the main differences being in the shape, size, colour and flavour of the fruit that they produce. This means that the advice given for growing blackberries can also be applied to the hybrid berries, and other rubus species.

Blackberries and hybrid berries can be eaten raw as part of a late summer fruit platter, but many fruit growers consider them to be at their best when cooked in a fruit compote or pie. Blackberries have a natural affinity with apples, and a handful of blackberries can enliven the filling of an apple pie, or they can be stuffed into an apple and baked. Blackberry jam is a classic, and a really good way of preserving the fruit. *Rubus* fruit freezes well and this method of preserving can be used to bring the taste of summer into the cold of the winter.

Planning

Probably the most important consideration when planning the planting of a blackberry or hybrid berry is the availability of sufficient space. With some varieties capable of putting on up to 4m (more than 12ft) of thorny new growth in a season, space can become a real issue. For most blackberries or hybrid berries this means that if more than one plant is to be grown, you will need to allow 2.4–3m (8–10ft) between plants. If there is not sufficient space, the plant will soon outgrow the situation and cultivation will become difficult. Indeed, it is the natural habit of a blackberry to grow through and over other shrubs and vegetation, a habit that the fruit grower must control if the plant is to be useful and productive.

Blackberries will ripen despite some shade, but to give the fruit a chance to ripen fully and develop the best flavour, choose a sunny aspect. Hybrid berries

OPPOSITE PAGE: **Raspberry *Autumn Bliss*.**

will really benefit from the sun when ripening – they may change colour and give the appearance of being ripe, but without sufficient sunshine they will remain sharp-tasting, as the sugars will have not developed. Try to choose a sheltered site where the plant will not

A selection of delicious soft fruit grown in the author's garden.

The blackberry is one of the most glorious cane fruits.

be exposed to cold winds which can damage young new growth.

Planting

Blackberries and hybrid berries are usually available in garden centres and nurseries already growing in containers. Plant in the autumn when the ground is still warm, or wait until spring. Prepare a shallow hole, adding some compost and a handful of a long-acting fertilizer like blood, fish and bone. Remove the plant from the container and spread out the roots, and cover with about 10cm (4in) of soil, keeping the soil at the same level as it was in the container – no deeper. Water in, and mulch over the area of the roots, keeping it just away from the growing canes. Start training the growing canes on to the wires, tying them just tightly enough to give support and prevent excessive movement in the wind, but not so tight as to restrict growth or the flow of water and nutrients up the canes to the growing tips.

Training and Support

Before planting blackberries or hybrid berries, it is advisable to prepare the site and decide how and where it will be trained and supported. In addition to growing extremely long and thorny canes, most blackberries and hybrid berries are 'floricane', which means they produce fruit on canes that have grown during the previous year. This means that at some time of the year the support that you are using will need to accommodate not just last year's canes, now fruiting, but also the new growing canes which will produce the fruit next year.

If the plant is to be grown against a wall or fence, try to choose one that is south- or southwest-facing. Next, a series of horizontal wires supported on vine eyes will need to be fixed across the space available, 30cm (12in) apart, starting from about 60cm (24in) up from the ground. Fix the top wire at a height that will be convenient for picking, probably about 1.8m (6ft) above ground level. In addition to fixing the vine eyes at each end of the wires, support may be needed in the middle if the wires are much more than 3m (10ft) long.

If a wall or fence is not available, and the plant is to be grown in an open space, it will need to be grown along a series of support wires, fixed to strong, upright posts or stakes. The direction in which the wires are run, and consequently the direction in which the growing plant faces, may be constrained by the shape and direction of the space available. This may mean that the wires have to be run in line with borders, paths or other garden features. However, in an open area, where the aspect and direction that the wires are to run in can be chosen, the wires could be run east–west to present the full width of the plant to the sun. However, this will produce a dense shady area behind the growing plant, which will shade other fruit. In general, if fruit is to be planted in rows, it is better to try to run support wires and posts in a north–south direction, and grow the plants in this plane. In this way each side of the plant will be in the sun for part of the day, and the shadow cast will be mini-

mized, enabling fruit to be grown in rows that get a more or less equal time in the sun. The space between rows will also be important: about 1.8–2.1m (6–7ft) is recommended between rows of blackberries.

Given optimum space, strong posts of about 7.5–10cm (3–4in) square or diameter, by at least 2.4m (8ft) long, should be fixed into the ground vertically. These posts should be buried at least 60cm (2ft) down, leaving 1.8m (6ft) out of the ground. Depending on the firmness of the soil, the posts may need to be set in concrete or compacted stones and rubble, and braced with shorter posts angled from the ground to a point at about half the height of the main posts. The posts need to be fixed securely, as once the plant is trained on the wires stretched between the posts, there will be quite a large area of leaf that will act like a sail as the wind blows, putting great pressure on the wires and posts. If there is to be a row of blackberry plants, the posts should be set about 2.4–3m (8–10ft) apart. To train the plants, galvanized wire of 1.6mm diameter (16 gauge) should be fixed

Strong wires are required to support heavy fruiting blackberries.

between the main posts, 30cm (12in) apart, starting from about 60cm (24in) up from the ground. Fix the top wire at a height that will be convenient for picking, probably 1.8m (6ft) above ground level. The wire should be stretched, tensioned and fixed firmly, as it will be under great strain when supporting a large blackberry plant laden with fruit.

Once the posts-and-wire system has been set up, there are a number of different ways in which blackberries and hybrid berries can be trained. Remember that most blackberries and hybrid berries will bear fruit on canes that were produced during the previous season. This means that, once established, a growing blackberry will consist of last year's canes that are flowering and bearing fruit, plus a series of new canes that are coming from the same growing point and will carry fruit for the next year. Ideally, the new canes should be allowed to grow unhindered, and tied out of the way of the old canes. This means that the

old canes do not become crowded and the fruit has space to develop and ripen. Also, the old canes can be removed safely without damaging the new canes, once fruiting is over. Away from the old canes, the new canes can grow freely, and are less likely to get tangled up with the old canes, or damaged.

There are a number of training systems that can be used to achieve this. Choose the one that best suits the space available.

Fan: planted midway between a pair of posts, the canes are spread out in a rough fan shape, with a more or less equal space between each cane. As they grow, radiating out from the centre of the fan shape, leave a space through the centre of the fan for the following year's new canes. Each cane is tied to the wires as it grows. Once they reach the top wire, the canes may be grown along the wire, or cut at a height/length that is convenient. These canes will produce the fruit

Blackberries trained in the alternate form.

Informally trained loganberries can produce a good crop.

next year. During the following year the old canes, the original fan shape, remain in place while they flower and fruit, and are then removed as soon as fruiting has finished, by cutting at ground level and being carefully removed from the wires. At the same time the new canes are trained vertically, as they grow, loosely bundling them up through the centre of the fan. They may be kept in this loose bundle through the winter to give some protection to the new young growing tips. The following spring these canes are then fanned out, as before, spacing them more or less equally, leaving the centre free for the next crop of new canes that will soon start to emerge. This pattern is repeated each year.

Alternate: this form of training involves tying all the canes produced one year in the same direction across the wires, say to the left of the point where the plant emerges from the ground. As the new canes grow during the following year, they are trained and tied in the opposite direction, to the right of the plant. This will keep the old canes to the left and the new canes

to the right, completely separate from each other. This reduces the risk of damage to the new canes while fruit is being picked from the old canes, and means that the old canes can be removed more easily, without coming anywhere near the new canes. Once they have been removed, the left-hand space is ready for the new canes that will emerge the following year, when the canes on the right become the 'old canes' and are fruited and removed. In this way the new growth changes from left to right in alternate years.

Informal: the vigorous nature of blackberries and hybrid berries means that the canes can be trained informally against fences or any other structures to which the plant can be tied, to support the canes and make picking easier. They can be grown in restricted areas, too, by winding the canes back and forth across the available space as they grow. Try to keep the canes spread out so that there is some air circulation around the fruit to help reduce the chance of mildew. The main thing is to make sure that the new growth each year can be identified, and kept out of the way of the old canes. Once fruiting has finished, the old canes are removed at ground level, leaving space for the new canes to be tied in.

Containers

Growing blackberries or other cane fruit in containers is certainly possible, but their rampant growth habit and sharp prickles can make the management of the container and its contents quite difficult. However, the airy and flexible nature of blackberry canes means that they can be woven round canes or a willow support structure in the container, as they grow, to great decorative effect. Ideally, the container should be relatively large, 40–50cm (16–20in) across the top, 50 litres or more, to allow for the development of the canes and sufficient watering. For the planting medium, use a mixture of 80 per cent peat-free compost, ericaceous for preference, plus 20 per cent loam-based potting compost, such as John Innes no. 2; add some grit to aid drainage. Make sure that the container is kept watered (but not waterlogged), and use rainwater if available as this will help keep the compost slightly acid, which is beneficial for blackberries. Fruit in containers will need feeding more than fruit in the ground, as the nutrients will wash through the container and out as it is watered, so add a slow-release fertilizer when mixing the compost, and water regularly with a high potash tomato fertilizer as soon as the fruits are set. Support the growing and fruiting blackberries with garden string tied to a bamboo cane in the centre of the container, or garden string tied round a series of bamboo canes pushed in around the edge of the container.

Look out for vine weevil infestation in the container – the signs include weak growth that does not respond to watering, small white grubs in the compost, or adult vine weevils crawling about on the plants after dark. Hand select and dispose of grubs and adults, and treat containers with a vine weevil nematode if a problem is suspected.

Cultivation

Blackberries and hybrid berries are best grown in the ground, but most plants available from garden centres will be bought in containers. Container-grown plants are available through the year and can be planted at more or less any time, but avoid planting after the fruit has set, as there is a good chance that it will be lost as the plant goes into shock as a result of replanting. The best time to buy and plant is when they are dormant, after leaf fall in the autumn and before the new buds open in the early spring. Planting can be done whenever the ground is accessible and not too wet, from autumn, when the ground is still warm, through to spring. If planted before the winter the canes can remain loosely tied in a bundle, to help protect the growing tips from frost. The canes should be unbundled, trained and tied to the support wires in the spring. Pruning will not be required while the canes are in a bundle, but when the bundle is untied any particularly weak or damaged canes can be removed.

The fruit of most blackberries and other hybrid berries is produced on the previous year's canes, a fruiting pattern known as *floricane*. This means that no pruning should be done in the spring as it will remove the canes that should be producing the crop of fruit. Once the fruit has been picked, the old canes should be cut out at ground level, and removed. The only exception to this is if the blackberry is one of the new *primocane* varieties that are available from some growers; primocane blackberries will produce fruit in the same way as autumn-fruiting raspberries. This means that the fruit is produced on canes that grow during the spring and early summer of the current year. Primocane blackberries should be cut low to the ground in the late winter each year.

Cultivation of floricane blackberries and hybrid berries is based on looking after and tending the new canes as they grow each year, and removing the old canes after the fruit has been picked, making room for the new canes which will fruit next year. Cultivation of the new primocane varieties is based on cutting down the old canes that fruited last year in late winter, and encouraging new canes to grow through the spring and early summer to produce this year's fruit crop.

Cane fruit will benefit from mulching in the spring

Reuben primocane blackberry.

Propagation is very easy. Exploiting the natural habit of cane fruits, take 'tip cuttings' – peg down the end of a growing cane, either into the ground or, for convenience, into a 10cm (4in) 1 litre pot of loam-based compost. The tip will soon take root and the new plant can be severed from the original cane once the roots have become established. Replant the new cutting where required.

Pruning

Newly planted blackberries will not generally require any pruning while the canes are in a bundle, but when the bundle is untied any particularly weak or damaged canes should be removed.

The pruning of floricane blackberries and other hybrid berries consists of cutting and removing the old canes at ground level after the fruit has been picked, making room for the new canes which will

Base of loganberry showing darker old canes which should be removed after fruiting and the lighter coloured canes of this year's growth for next year's fruit.

to keep the root area moist; water in dry conditions to help maintain strong, healthy new growth and nice juicy fruit. It will also benefit from a general purpose fertilizer in the spring, and feeding with high potash fertilizer once the fruit has set.

As the plants age, they may start to show signs of fungal or virus problems. These can be managed to some degree, but once the plant becomes unhealthy and unproductive, it is best to dig it up and dispose of it. It is good practice to replace cane fruit with new, healthy stock every ten years or so, planting in a different part of the garden to reduce the chance of any infection being transferred to the new plants. If there is no opportunity for resiting the cane fruit, the soil around the roots should be replaced with new, fresh soil that is less likely to contain fungal spores that can cause problems.

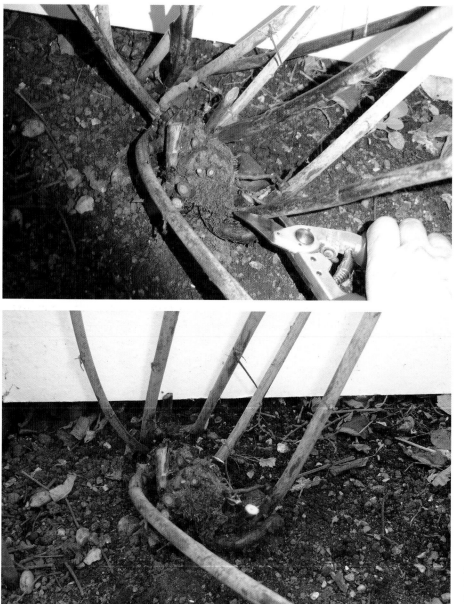

Pruning out the old (dark-coloured) canes.

After pruning, leave the new canes for next year's fruit.

fruit next year. Any weak or damaged canes can be removed in the spring when the bundles of canes are untied after the winter and trained into their fruiting position. The tips of these canes can be removed if they are too long and cannot be tied into the available wires or framework of supports.

The old canes of primocane varieties that fruited last year should be cut down in late winter, to encourage new canes to grow through the spring and early summer to produce this year's fruit crop.

Pests, Diseases and Problems

Blackberries can suffer from problems that affect all fruit, but there are a number of pests and diseases that are specific to blackberries. Listed below are common problems; please refer to the Pests, Diseases and Problems section within Chapter 4.

Aphids
Birds and beasts
Drought
Frost
Fungal diseases (Cane blight, Cane spot, Purple blotch, Spur blight)
Grey mould
Phytophthora
Raspberry beetle
Vine weevil
Virus disease

Recommended Varieties

There are many varieties of blackberry to choose from, from the traditional thorny ones through to the newer thornless varieties. AGM indicates that the variety has won an RHS Award of Garden Merit.

Adrienne: thornless canes, good flavour, attractive double pink flowers. Season: early.

Black Butte: many claims, mostly justified, are made for the large size of fruit that can be grown on this variety, which also has a good flavour; relatively vigorous canes that can stand up to the cold in winter. Season: early.

Loch Ness (AGM): large tasty fruit, and canes are thornless so easy to handle; relatively compact habit yet produces a heavy crop; some resistance to purple blotch. Season: mid.

Oregon Thornless: medium-sized juicy fruit, mild flavour; well liked for its attractive, finely divided, fern-like leaves. Season: mid to late.

Ruben: the first generally available primocane blackberry; claimed to produce large succulent fruit, but it is too new to draw conclusions about its long-term performance, and garden trials suggest that it needs a warm climate, which may mean that it is more suitable for growing in the south of the country; however, its habit of fruiting on new canes produced in the current season makes it relatively easy to grow and a valuable addition to the fruit garden. Season: late.

Oregon Thornless blackberry with its distinctive fern-like leaves.

Sylvan (AGM): vigorous and thorny, but large, good-flavoured fruit. Season: early.

Waldo: relatively new, thornless variety; large, firm, good-quality fruit, ideal for jam-making; some resistance to cane spot and purple blotch, but canes are somewhat brittle and easily damaged by wind if they are not tied in early. Season: very early.

There are a number of varieties of hybrid berries (blackberry x raspberry crosses) that are worth growing.

Boysenberry: with the taste of wild brambles, but with consistently large juicy fruit; more tolerant of dry soil than some of the other cane fruit. Season: mid.

Loganberry – Thornless LY 654 (AGM): this variety is the most widely available, and quite rightly, as it is a reliable cropper, producing large fruits with a rich, distinctive flavour; resist picking fruits as soon as they turn bright red, as they will be too sharp to enjoy – leave to hang until dark red to purple, and pick just before the skin gets too full of juice to handle. Season: successional picking through July and August. A thorny loganberry *LY 59* (AGM) is available at some nurseries and garden centres; it crops well and has a good flavour that is very distinctive. Season: successional picking through July and August.

Tayberry (AGM): large, sweet, yet mild-flavoured fruit that is perfect for jam; leave to hang until dark red. The Medana tayberry cultivar is certified to be virus-free. Season: early.

Tummelberry: large, aromatic red fruit; canes are moderately vigorous; said to be more winter hardy than the tayberry. Season: mid.

Thornless *LY 654* loganberry.

Blackcurrant (*Ribes nigrum*)

Ben Sarek blackcurrant.

Blackcurrants are really easy to grow, repaying good feeding with a heavy crop. They have many uses, cooked in pies and tarts and as an essential ingredient for summer puddings, providing colour, flavour and a rich, dark juice that soaks into the pudding. They may be eaten raw for dessert, or made into jams or cordials. Blackcurrants have a strong and distinctive flavour and are reported to contain high levels of vitamin C and antioxidants. The leaves of blackcurrants are extremely aromatic and can be used to flavour sorbets or to make an interesting cordial in their own right.

Left alone, blackcurrants will grow as a large, sprawling bush, but more compact varieties are available to suit whatever space is available in the garden. The size of fruit varies by variety, and blackcurrants have benefited from modern commercial breeding programmes which have resulted in larger fruits, some growing to the size of marbles, and higher levels of vitamins and fruit sugars, which means that they require less added sweetener than some of the older varieties.

Planting

Blackcurrants need sun to ripen the fruit and develop the flavours and sugar levels. While they will grow with some shade, the more sun they can be exposed to the better the quality of the fruit.

Blackcurrants are best grown as stooled bushes – that is, bushes where the new shoots come straight out of the ground, rather than radiating out from a central leg or trunk.

Start with a deep hole that has some nitrogen-rich compost, such as farmyard manure, mixed into the bottom of it. Sprinkle a long-term fertilizer such as blood, fish and bone over the soil that is to be used to back-fill the hole. New bushes, bought in containers, should be planted in a hole that is deeper than the original container; if they are bare rooted, they should be planted deeper than the level at which they were growing in the nursery. This is done to encourage the new fruit-bearing branches to grow from the base of the plant, below ground level.

Back-fill and firm in the soil around the roots. Top-dress with compost or farmyard manure to retain moisture in the soil and to maintain the high levels of nitrogen that blackcurrants need to thrive. Try not to let the compost remain in contact with the branches as they emerge from the soil, as this may encourage soil-borne fungal problems to take hold. Water well at planting, and make sure that the plant does not dry out before it gets a chance to start growing new shoots.

Plants should be given space to grow and flourish. Allow 1.2–1.5m (4–5ft) between bushes if you have room; if not, choose one of the more compact growers, such as *Ben Sarek*.

Blackcurrants can be grown in containers, in soil-based potting compost with some grit added to improve drainage. Container-grown plants will need regular feeding and top-dressing, and unless the container is large, it can prove difficult to keep up the cultivation regime that encourages replacement branches from the base of the plant, and the fruit crop will be small.

Look out for vine weevil infestation in the container: signs include weak growth that does not respond to watering, small white grubs in the compost, and adult vine weevils crawling about on the plants after dark. Hand select and dispose of grubs and adults, and treat containers with a vine weevil nematode if a problem is suspected.

Training and Support

Newly planted blackcurrants do not usually require any additional support if they are well firmed in. As they grow, the replacement branches that emerge from below ground level will help to anchor and stabilize the plant.

During the summer support may be required for individual branches that are carrying a heavy crop of fruit. This is done not only to prevent the branch breaking and damaging the plant, but also to lift the fruit up from ground level and allow more air to get to the fruit to help ripening. To do this, individual branches may be supported by a cane, or the 'Maypoling' technique could be used. Maypoling means inserting a sturdy cane or stake into the ground near the centre of the bush, then supporting branches individually with strings that run from each branch to the top of the cane, giving the overall appearance of a maypole.

Generally, blackcurrants do not tend to be trained in any of the decorative forms as the fruiting wood is removed each year and new replacement growth must be encouraged for next year's fruit.

Cultivation

Blackcurrants are grown as stooled bushes; these are bushes where the main branches grow straight out of the ground, rather than from a single stem, like gooseberries. The plants are described as 'gross feeders', which means that they need high levels of nitrogen-rich feed to stimulate the new growth required each year for the production of fruit. Container-growing is possible, but it is difficult to keep the plant well enough fed to produce the new growth required.

New plants are available through the year and can be planted at more or less any time, but avoid planting once the fruit has set, as there is a good chance that it will be lost as the plant goes into shock as a result of the replanting. The best time to buy and plant is when they are dormant, after leaf fall in the autumn and before the new buds open in the early spring. Planting can be done whenever the ground is accessible and not too wet, from autumn through to spring. Little formative pruning is usually required at planting; simply remove any damaged shoots or branches that are crossing into the centre of the bush.

Pruning

The majority of the fruit on blackcurrants is produced on one-year-old wood – that is, the new shoots that have grown one year and ripened over the winter. This means that this year's new growth will produce fruit next year. Consequently, is important to keep a succession of new growth being produced each year by the plant. If the new growth does not happen, or if it is removed, there will be no fruit. New growth is fairly easy to spot – clean young shoots emerging from the base of the plant, or new laterals growing from older branches that had been left unpruned, being a much paler colour than the old wood. Pruning for fruit is an important part of cultivation for blackcurrants. The idea is to stimulate and encourage vigorous

Blackcurrants are best grown as stooled bushes, the branches growing straight out of the ground.

new growth each year. This pruning should be done during the summer when the fruit is ripe, and consists of cutting out entire branches of old wood, with fruit still attached, either at ground level or above a bud or new lateral on a main branch. The fruit can then be picked from the branches in comfort, away from the bushes. It may be useful to place sheets of newspaper under the bushes when pruning in this way to collect any fruit that falls off during pruning. The removal of entire fruit-covered branches will open up the bush. This approach, combined with high nitrogen feeds, means new buds will be stimulated into growth and new shoots should emerge from below ground level. It is on this new growth that next year's crop will be formed. Up to one-third of the old fruiting branches can be removed each year to keep the blackcurrant bushes healthy and productive.

Winter pruning consists of removing any dead, diseased or badly positioned branches that can be seen when the leaves have fallen.

Blackcurrant crops have been affected badly as winters have got shorter, and are rarely as cold as fruit growers have experienced in the past. To produce a good crop of fruit, blackcurrant plants need to hibernate, requiring a minimum period of winter chill of 2000 hours at temperatures below 6°C to produce to their full potential. If the weather does not turn cold enough, this is difficult to manage for domestic fruit growing, short of moving north or to a colder country, but blackcurrant crops will be disappointing if the plants fail to get sufficient winter chilling through natural weather conditions.

During flowering bushes should be protected with horticultural fleece if frost is forecast. The flowers are insect-pollinated, but the flowers are often open on cold days in early spring when there are few insects about. There is some benefit in sheltering the plants from any cold easterly winds that will make it difficult for pollinating insects to do their job. Once the flowers have been pollinated and the fruit has set, clusters of tiny blackcurrants will be seen on the branches. These will swell quickly if there is sufficient rain; if not, watering may be necessary.

Established blackcurrant bushes require lots of feeding to keep them producing new fruiting growth.

A proportion of the darker older wood is pruned out during the summer to leave the new light-coloured shoots for next year's fruit.

During the winter prune for tidiness, leaving the previous year's new growth which carries the fruit buds for this year's fruit.

Apply a general purpose fertilizer with a high level of nitrogen, such as pelleted poultry manure, during the autumn and spring. An alternative way of introducing additional nitrogen to the ground around blackcurrants is to sow winter tares as green manure in the early autumn; let it grow over the winter, then hoe off the green top growth in the spring. This particular green manure will fix nitrogen in the soil around the roots of the blackcurrants and the hoed-off tops will provide mulch in the spring. Take care not to hoe too deeply, risking damage to the roots of the blackcurrant bush. The early spring is also a good time to apply sulphate of potash, if required. Once the fruit has set, a high-potash tomato fertilizer can be applied to help the fruit develop. Blackcurrant plants will produce fruit within their first year, although it is advisable to remove these to encourage the development of a stronger root system. Fruiting will be at its best after three or four years. The plants will live for over twenty

Ben Connan blackcurrant.

years, but fruit production will decline unless new, replacement growth is encouraged through winter pruning.

Propagation can be done by taking hard-wood cuttings in the autumn.

Newly planted blackcurrants may require some initial formative pruning to remove any crossing or damaged branches and to start to get the plant to grow into the required shape. Summer pruning is important for blackcurrants to stimulate and encourage the new growth that will produce fruit next year – this is described in detail in the Cultivation section above.

Pests, Diseases and Problems

Blackcurrants can suffer from problems that affect all fruit, but there are a number of pests and diseases that are specific to blackcurrants. Listed below are common problems; please refer to the Pests, Diseases and Problems section within Chapter 4.

American gooseberry mildew
Aphids
Big bud mite
Birds and beasts
Coral spot
Drought
Frost
Honey fungus
Phytophthora
Reversion
Vine weevil

Recommended Varieties

There are quite a few varieties of blackcurrant, some older types that are tried and tested, plus lots of new introductions that benefit from having larger, juicier fruit.

Baldwin: an old favourite that was bred in the UK well over a hundred years ago; it remains popular because it has a milder flavour than some others, yet is just as high in Vitamin C. Season: mid to late.

Wellington XXX: another old UK variety, a vigorous grower, producing a good crop of tasty fruit. Season: mid.

The modern '*Ben ...*' varieties bred by the Scottish Crop Research Institute are all reliable and have been selected for their resistance to common problems that affect blackcurrants. Particularly useful varieties include:

Ben Connan (AGM): large tasty fruit on strigs that are long for blackcurrants, and win prizes regularly in fruit competitions; compact grower, some resistance to American gooseberry mildew. Season: early to mid.

Ben Hope: a new, vigorous grower, with some resistance to big bud mite and mildew; good flavour and a heavy cropper. Season: late.

Ben Sarek (AGM): large, marble-sized, juicy fruit with a good flavour; bush relatively compact and upright, which is useful if there is only a small space to grow blackcurrants. Shows some resistance to American gooseberry mildew, which has been known to cause problems for some varieties of blackcurrant. One of the hardier varieties, it also which shows some resistance to frost. Season: early to mid.

Ben Sarek blackcurrant.

Blueberry (*Vaccinium*)

Blueberries are new to many gardeners but they can be grown relatively easily if the conditions are right.

Native cousins of the blueberry, known as blaeberry, whortleberry, wimberry and other local names, grow wild in many parts of Britain, and cultivated varieties of blueberry have been grown commercially in the UK for over fifty years, but it is only in recent times that the fruit has become popular with amateur fruit growers. Its rise in popularity has been linked with research that suggests the health-giving properties of the fruit. Hailed in some quarters as a 'superfruit', it contains high levels of antioxidants as well as Vitamins A, B, C and E, and a range of vital trace elements, similar, in fact, to other black- and blue-skinned berried

fruits; claims have also been made that, if eaten regularly, blueberries are beneficial for reducing problems associated with a wide range of mental and physical health issues. As a result, commercial growers have experienced a boom in demand, and retailers have been quick to maximize the profit they can make on selling this fruit – which means that they are often very expensive to buy. All these are excellent reasons why you might consider growing blueberries yourself. Blueberries are something of an acquired taste; they are certainly milder than blackcurrants, but they can be eaten raw as a snack without the need for additional sweetening, or mixed into a fruit smoothie, and they make a very nice addition to any summer fruit salad or compote.

Blueberry buds ready to burst in the spring.

In addition to producing lovely fruit, a blueberry also deserves a place in any garden as a decorative shrub. It produces masses of attractive, scented, white flowers in the spring, and the leaves of most varieties produce good autumn colour.

Planting

Blueberries are sometimes described as 'heathland plants', which means that in the wild this kind of plant would be found growing in exposed, open sites, where the soil is low in nutrients, relatively infertile, free-draining, often sandy and tending to be acidic. In a garden situation, position blueberries where they will get as much sun as possible; although they will thrive in light shade, the fruit may not ripen well. Plants should be kept damp but without getting waterlogged, or the fruit will not grow to a decent size. Shelter from strong winds that could damage the plant. Grown to maturity, after eight or ten years a blueberry bush can reach 1.2–1.5m (4–5ft) high, and 1.2m (4ft) across, so ideally plants need to be spaced 1.5m (5ft) apart.

New bushes, bought in containers, should be planted in a large hole, prepared with compost, at the same level as the compost in the container. Mulch well after planting.

The popularity of blueberries means that plants are widely available in pots in garden centres, and the way they are sold might lead you to think that they are an easy fruit to grow. This may, indeed, be true in some areas, but blueberries require particular soil conditions to grow successfully, and if these are not maintained the fruit crop will be disappointing. The key thing to remember is that blueberries must be grown in what is known as 'acid soil'; this means soil with a pH value of between 4 and 5.5 (pH is the chemical measurement of acidity). Blueberries also require soil that is well drained, and do best in areas with relatively high rainfall in the summer.

Basically, if rhododendrons or azaleas grow successfully in your garden without the need to condition the soil, it will probably have the right pH for growing blueberries; just check that it is well drained and does not get waterlogged over winter. Conversely, if lilacs and pink hydrangeas grow well in your garden and the surrounding area, or if the ground is described as 'chalky', it indicates that the soil is probably 'alkaline' (with a pH value of 7.0 or higher) and is therefore not suitable for growing blueberries.

In the short term garden soil can be made more acidic by the addition of chemicals or lots of organic

If rhododendrons grow well, the acidity level of the soil will be suitable for blueberry cultivation.

matter and mulching with pine needles, but it will quickly revert to its original pH level, water will seep into the roots from areas that have not been treated, and acid-loving plants like the blueberry will soon start to show signs of mineral deficiencies, such as severely yellowing leaves. In this situation the plant will decline rapidly and no worthwhile fruit will be produced.

The only way to be certain about the pH of your soil is to test it. DIY kits are available at most garden centres, or you can have it tested by a soil-testing laboratory. The key thing about testing is to take samples from different places in the garden to get an overall picture, rather than test just one spot that may not be typical of the garden as a whole.

If the soil is within the pH range suitable for growing blueberries (4 to 5.5), then they can be planted into the garden. If not, alternatives must be considered.

Raised beds: these can be constructed using timber, brick or other material that will be strong enough to hold its shape when filled with compost. Used for growing blueberries, a raised bed will need to have sides that are at least 45cm (18in) deep. The size will depend on the space available, but remember that a full-grown high-bush blueberry could take up an area up to 1.2m by 1.2m (4ft by 4ft). Cover the base of the bed (the original level of the garden soil) with a single sheet of heavy-duty black polythene large enough to come at least 15cm (6in) up the sides of the bed; this

helps to prevent water of the wrong pH filtering into the raised bed. If the sides are made of solid material, drainage holes will need to be made to prevent waterlogging. Once constructed and lined, the raised bed must be filled with an ericaceous (acidic) compost and plenty of garden compost and organic matter; horticultural grit should also be added to improve drainage. Help the compost to settle by tamping or watering lightly with rainwater. The blueberry plants should be planted into the ericaceous compost at the same level that they were growing in their pots. Plants in a raised bed will need to be irrigated as they will not be able to take up water from the garden.

One alternative to making a raised bed for blueberries is a sunken bed, dug down to a similar depth, 45cm (18in), into the garden itself; again line the hole with heavy-duty black polythene, but bring the edge

Blueberry growing in a plastic barrel of acid compost which has been sunk into the ground.

up and out of the hole so that water cannot run in across the surface; prick the polythene across the base of the hole to provide drainage. Fill the sunken bed with ericaceous compost, organic matter and horticultural grit to aid drainage. The pH level in this kind of sunken bed will need to be maintained through regular mulching, and may need to be treated from time to time with a soil acidifier such as sulphate of iron (ferrous sulphate), as water from the surrounding area can enter the sunken bed and raise the pH. Use rainwater to maintain moisture at the roots during dry spells.

Container growing: this may be the best option for gardeners with soil that is not sufficiently acidic. A single fully grown blueberry will ultimately require a pot or container that holds about 50–70 litres of compost (a pot that is about 45cm (18in) across the top and 45cm high); of course, when starting off with a small plant, the container can also be smaller, increasing the size by repotting as the plant grows. The container must be filled with ericaceous compost, with added grit to help drainage. Never let the compost dry out; water with rainwater to keep the compost moist, but do not allow it to become waterlogged. Blueberries grown in containers will need feeding more than fruit in the ground, as the nutrients will wash out through the container as it is watered. Feed in the spring with a fertilizer that is suitable for rhododendrons and azaleas, such as sulphate of iron, and with a high-potash tomato fertilizer once the fruit has set.

Look out for vine weevil infestation in the container – signs include weak growth that does not respond to watering, small white grubs in the compost, and adult vine weevils crawling about on the plants after dark. Hand select and dispose of grubs and adults, and treat containers with a vine weevil nematode if a problem is suspected.

Training and Support

Newly planted blueberries do not usually require any additional support if they are well firmed-in. Generally, blueberries do not tend to be trained in any of the decorative forms.

Growing blueberries in containers means that you can choose the perfect compost.

Cultivation

Blueberries are best grown as stooled bushes – that is, bushes where the new shoots come straight out of the ground, rather than radiating out from a central leg or trunk. The ground should be kept damp, mulching each spring with acidic organic matter such as pine needles or conifer bark, but try to prevent mulch from coming into contact with the bush itself, as this will reduce the chance of a soil-based fungal infection, such as Phytophthora, from attacking the plant. Feed plants each spring with a balanced fertilizer that is suitable for ericaceous plants such as rhododendrons and azaleas. Do not use any fertilizer that could be on the alkaline side of the pH range, such as spent mushroom compost. Blueberries have a mass of surface roots, so take care not to delve too deep when weeding around the plants or when applying fertilizer as these could get damaged. Water with rainwater when available, especially in areas where the mains water is known to be hard or chalky, but any water is

better than no water during dry periods. Blueberries must be kept damp but not waterlogged if they are to put on sufficient new growth and produce a crop of worthwhile fruits.

Fruit on blueberries does not ripen all at once, but will be spread out over a period of time. This means that you can have several pickings off the same bush. Try not to pick too soon, when the skin starts to colour, as the berry itself will not have ripened and the flavour will not have developed. Be patient and wait for the colour to deepen through different shades of blue; test one every now and again, and pick once the fruit has matured.

Ripe blueberries ready for picking, with more to come.

Do not expect much fruit in the first few years, as blueberry bushes do not come into full production until they become mature, at eight to ten years old, by which time they may be 1–1.2m high (3–4ft).

Pruning

Blueberries are unlikely to require any pruning for the

first two or three years, other than tidying up after the winter, as they will need to grow and get established before any wood is removed. Blueberries will start to produce fruit on new wood that has grown the previous summer, so once the blueberry is established, the aim of pruning is to stimulate the production of new growth from the base of the plant. This can be achieved by removing a proportion of the oldest wood that is over three years old. Remove no more than a quarter of the oldest wood in any one year, cutting back to the base of the plant or to a new bud on a strong upright branch, in the late winter. Worthwhile quantities of fruit will also be produced

on one-year-old side shoots from wood that is two or three years old; remove this and you will remove the potential to fruit. After the winter bushes may need a tidy-up to remove any dead wood and branches that have been damaged or are crossing over. Weak spindly growth or branches that trail on to the ground can also be removed. However, if the plant is producing a good crop there may be no need to prune much at all, other than keeping it tidy, but leave no wood that is more than six years old.

Fertilization

Most blueberries are described as self-fertile, meaning that the flower should not require fertilization from another blueberry to produce fruit, and you should get fruit from a single plant. However, fertilization levels, and therefore the size of the crop, can be improved by growing two different varieties of blueberry so that they will cross-pollinate and produce a better fruit set, and consequently a better crop.

Pests, Diseases and Problems

Blueberries can suffer from problems that affect all fruit, but there are a number of pests and diseases that are specific to blueberries. Listed below are common problems; please refer to the Pests, Diseases and Problems section within Chapter 4.

Birds and beasts
Coral spot
Drought
Frost
Honey fungus
Phytophthora
Vine weevil

Recommended Varieties

Although most blueberries are described as being self-fertile, one plant growing on its own will not be as productive as if two different varieties are grown

Blueberry *Bluecrop*.

Blueberry *Duke*.

together – cross-fertilization will improve and increase the quality and quantity of the crop.

Berkeley: large, light blue fruits, mild and very sweet, on a large, spreading and very productive bush. Season: mid.

Bluecrop: large sweet fruit, on a large bush if left to grow to its full potential. Season: early.

Duke (AGM): late flowering, which may help avoid frost damage, yet ripening relatively early in the season; medium to large-sized, well flavoured fruit. Season: early.

Herbert: considered by some growers to have one of the best flavours, it grows vigorously and produces clusters of large berries; attractive pink flower buds. Season: mid.

Patriot: reliable cropper, good size, good flavour, low growing, spreading bush with brilliant autumn colour; some resistance to Phytophthora, root rot. Season: early.

Spartan (AGM): medium-sized fruit with good flavour; crops well if grown with a second variety as a pollinator, particularly good autumn colour. Season: early to mid.

Gooseberry (*Ribes uva-crispa*)

For many, the word gooseberry conjures up memories of a fruit that is small, hard, green and sour – but when you grow your own, it need not be so. It is a fruit that can surprise – indeed, with the gooseberry there are many more choices than for some other fruit. Gooseberries can produce fruits that range in size from just few grams to monsters that weigh in at over 50g each. While it is true that most gooseberries start off green, and indeed some stay a deep shade of green, there are varieties that ripen to yellow, red or white with a hint of green.

Like any fruit picked before it is ripe, a raw gooseberry will taste sharp or sour. Some cooks value this tartness for the production of sauces to accompany meat or fish. Early picked gooseberries will be firm and won't collapse if cooked gently, so are ideal for pies or tarts, but they may need some sugar to make them more palatable. Left to ripen on the bush, a gooseberry will develop sugar levels close to that of grapes and will taste very sweet, becoming a lovely dessert fruit that can be eaten raw without the need for additional sugar. Some varieties, like *Langley Gage* or *Lancashire Lad*, have distinct flavours when ripe and are very tasty.

Planting

Gooseberries are a woodland fruit, so are quite happy growing with some shade. In fact, long periods of hot sun can damage gooseberry fruit and leaves by scorching. One factor that will help to produce good crops of gooseberries is air flow – planting where they will receive a good blow. A good air flow helps to reduce the occurrence of American gooseberry mildew, and provides conditions that are not liked by adult gooseberry sawfly, so they will be encouraged to lay their

ABOVE: *Lancashire Lad* **gooseberries ripening from green to red.**

LEFT: **Gooseberries – yellow, red, green and white.**

eggs elsewhere. It will also aid pollination, as insects may be scarce in the cold air when the gooseberries come into flower.

When planting new gooseberries, the soil should be kept at the same level as it was in the nursery or the container – no deeper, as you do not want to encourage new shoots from below ground level. The same applies with bare-rooted plants – keep the soil at the same level that the plant was at in the nursery.

Newly planted gooseberries will benefit from being given support by tying to a cane inserted into the ground about 7.5cm (3in) from the plant, avoiding its roots if possible. If there is a row of cordon gooseberries, the canes can be tied to wires for additional support.

Gooseberries can be successfully grown in containers, as long as the roots have sufficient room and the container is kept watered – but not waterlogged. Use an open, soil-based potting compost with added grit for best results. Fruit in containers will need feeding more than fruit in the ground, as the nutrients will wash out through the container as it is watered.

Look out for vine weevil infestation in the container – signs include weak growth that does not respond to watering, small white grubs in the compost, and adult vine weevils crawling about on the plants after dark. Hand select and dispose of grubs and adults, and treat containers with a vine weevil nematode if a problem is suspected.

Training

There are a number of ways to grow gooseberries; select the one that suits the space available or the shape you want.

Bush: this is the traditional shape, and is likely to be the basic form in which you buy a new gooseberry plant. Even though it is shaped like a bush, the gooseberry should be grown on a single leg, a length of bare plant between the ground and where the branches start, about 25–30cm (10–12in) above ground level. This provides air flow under the bush, and helps to make sure that branches laden with fruit do not drag on the ground and get dirty from rain splash or

eaten by slugs and the like. Having space below the branches will also make picking easier – the branches of most gooseberries are covered with vicious thorns, but if the bush is encouraged to produce horizontal branches the fruit will hang down for easier picking.

Viewed from above, a gooseberry bush should have four or five main horizontal branches radiating out from the main stem. It is good practice to try to prune a bush-grown gooseberry into an 'open cup' shape. This means cutting out any vertical growth from the centre of the bush, but leaving new growth around the outer circumference.

Grown in an unrestricted way in a garden with plenty of space, gooseberry bushes can be planted 1.5–1.8m (6–6ft) apart, and will grow to 1.5m (5ft) tall; allow about 1.5m (5ft) between rows. However, if space is at a premium, gooseberries can be planted closer together and trimmed so that the branches do not grow into each other. If space is really tight, consider growing gooseberries in a restricted form such as a cordon, so they can be planted close together and several plants can be grown in a relatively small space.

Standard: this means growing the bush shape higher up off the ground. The bush is simply lifted from ground level, up a long straight leg that can be 0.90–1.2m (3–4ft) high, to a height that means that the fruit can be picked without the need to bend down. A standard gooseberry can also be an attractive and unusual talking point. Standard gooseberries can be bought from nurseries and garden centres, ready trained; alternatively, you can grow your own standard gooseberry from a cutting or a single cordon plant, by removing all side shoots and allowing the central leader to continue growing upwards. When the central leader reaches beyond the height that you want, prune it back in the winter to a strong, upward-facing bud at the desired height. The new growth in the spring should start to produce branches that can be shaped as described for a bush. It is advisable to support standard-grown gooseberries with a stake or strong cane as a bush at the top of a single leg can become heavy and may be damaged, especially in heavy rain or strong winds.

Rows of single-cordon gooseberries in RHS Garden Wisley, Surrey.

Cordon: cordon growing is ideal for gooseberries as it provides a good air flow and makes fruit picking easy as the fruit hangs on short laterals, clear of spiny branches. A cordon is essentially a straight main branch growing vertically, tied to a cane or horizontal wires for support. A single cordon can be developed by allowing the central leader of a new cutting to continue growing upward, keeping the lateral shoots pruned to about 7.5cm (3in) in the winter, 15cm (6in) in the summer. Double or triple cordons can be developed by allowing a second or third vertical branch to grow up from about 25cm (10in) above soil level. Hard pruning the leader for a single cordon to an upward-facing bud at about this height in the winter will encourage strong new shoots in the spring, the strongest of which can be selected and trained up as vertical cordons. Unwanted shoots can be stopped by pruning them out and rubbing off any subsequent buds that form.

Gooseberries grown as single cordons can be planted as close as 30cm (12in) apart if you can keep on top of the pruning regime; if not, allow a little more room. Space double or triple cordons so that the new lateral growth does not grow together and provide a perfect environment for gooseberry sawfly larvae. A row of cordon gooseberries can be supported by canes, and tied to horizontal wires stretched between stout posts, spaced 60cm (24in) apart and 1.2m (4ft) from the ground. Allow about 1.5m (5ft), between rows of cordon gooseberries.

Gooseberries can also be trained in more decorative forms, such as fans, which can be grown on wires to cover a fence panel or wall. The basic principles of fan training are covered in Chapter 1.

Cultivation

Gooseberries may be planted in the ground or grown in containers. Container-grown plants are available through the year and can be planted at more or less any time, but avoid planting once the fruit has set as there is a good chance that it will be lost as the plant goes into shock as a result of the replanting. The best time to buy and plant is when the gooseberries are dormant, after leaf fall in the autumn and before the new buds open in the early spring. At this stage the shape and form of the plant can be seen clearly and any formative pruning required to shape the plant can be done easily. Planting can be done whenever the ground is accessible and not too wet, from autumn, when the ground is still warm, through to spring.

The fruit of gooseberries is produced from buds on ripe wood and around the base of the previous year's growth, so winter pruning is most important for fruit production to build up lots of fruiting spurs. This can be done any time after the leaves have fallen and the plant is dormant, say November, until growth starts again in March. It consists of cutting back previously summer-pruned laterals to above buds at about 7.5cm (3in) on bushes, or to 5cm (2in) on cordons. Because the fruit buds can be damaged by birds during the winter months as they search for aphids, it may be better to delay winter pruning on these fruit until as late as the middle of February. The leaders of the main branches of bush-grown plants are cut back by about half of last season's growth to a bud that is pointing upwards and outwards – this will produce new growth that is strong enough to support this year's fruit crop. On cordons, the leaders are cut back by up to half of the previous season's new growth to an upward-pointing bud to continue to encourage strong vertical growth. Once a cordon has reached the required height, cut back each winter to a bud at about this height. By pruning later in the winter, any damaged or crossing branches can be seen and removed by cutting back to sound and healthy wood. Look out for branches that have died back and are host to coral spot fungus – remove these by cutting back to healthy wood.

Flowering tends to be relatively early, and bushes should be protected with horticultural fleece if frost is forecast. The flowers are insect-pollinated, but the flowers are often open on cold days in early spring when there are few insects about. Pollination levels can be improved if there is a good air flow round the plants. Lightly tapping the branches when the flowers are open fully and the pollen is ripe helps to shake the pollen into the flowers.

Once the flowers have been pollinated and the fruit has set, small embryonic gooseberries will be seen on the branches. These will swell quickly if there is sufficient rain; if not, watering may be necessary.

Gooseberries may be thinned by removing a proportion of the small fruits, taking groups of berries down to single fruits spaced about 5cm (2in) apart, enabling them to swell to their full extent and ripen. The traditional time for pruning gooseberries is Whitsun, nowadays better known as the Spring Bank Holiday, at the end of May. The thinnings need not be thrown away, but with a little sweetening can be used for the first gooseberry pie of the season.

Established gooseberries require little feeding, just a light sprinkling of a general purpose fertilizer in the very early spring. Some gardeners find that rose

Embryo gooseberries soon after pollination.

fertilizer has a good balance of nutrients and trace elements that suit gooseberries. The early spring is also a good time to apply sulphate of potash if required; alternatively, apply a sprinkling of wood ash over the area of the roots, which can be produced by burning the wood removed during winter pruning. Avoid fertilizers with high levels of nitrogen on gooseberries, as this can encourage soft growth which tends to be more susceptible to American gooseberry mildew. In contrast, growing the plants 'hard' helps them resist this problem. Once the fruit has set, a tomato fertilizer that is high in potash can be applied to help the fruit develop. Gooseberries have relatively shallow root systems so will benefit from mulching with compost in the spring, to help retain the moisture in the soil surrounding the plants. Be careful when applying the mulch to avoid touching the leg of the plant with the compost. Keeping it clean by brushing the compost away will reduce the chance of a soil-based fungal infection, such as *Phytophthora*, from attacking the plant.

Gooseberry plants will produce fruit within their first year, although it is advisable to remove these to encourage the development of a stronger root system. Fruiting will be at its best after three or four years. The plants will live for over twenty years, but fruit production will decline unless new, replacement growth is encouraged through winter pruning.

Propagation can be done by taking hard-wood cuttings in the autumn.

Pruning

Newly planted gooseberries will require some initial formative pruning to remove any crossing or damaged branches and to start to get the plant to grow into the required shape. If growing as a bush, four or five well-spaced leaders radiating out from the leg should be selected and shortened by half, to an upward- and outward-pointing bud. Aim to produce a 'cup shape', with an open centre, with four or five main branches radiating out from the leg, with an open centre to the bush. Remove branches that are in the wrong place, cutting right back to the leg on which the bush will grow. Weak laterals can be removed, and the laterals that remain should be trimmed to a bud about 7.5cm (3in) out from the branch. If the new plant is to be trained as a cordon, the plant needs to be encouraged to put its energies into a single, strong, upright growth. Select the strongest upright growth and cut all other branches back to within 7.5cm (3in) of what will become the central leader; prune this leader back by up to half the length of the new growth that was made during the previous season to an upward-pointing bud that will produce strong new growth.

Gooseberries produce fruit buds on spurs, on ripe wood and around the base of the previous year's growth, so the aim of winter pruning is to establish a strong spur system on laterals on the main branches. The leaders of the main branches of bush-grown plants are cut back by about half of last season's growth to a bud that is pointing upwards and outwards – this will produce new growth that is strong enough to support this year's fruit crop and help stimulate the growth of strong branches and laterals. On cordons, the leaders are cut back by about half of the season's new growth on to an upward-pointing bud to encourage strong vertical growth. Once a cordon has reached the desired height, it can be kept at this height by pruning back the new growth each winter to just one bud. By pruning later in the winter, any damaged or crossing branches can be seen and removed by cutting back to sound and healthy wood. Look out for branches that have died back and are host to coral spot fungus – remove these by cutting back to healthy wood.

If the plant is being trained as a cordon, the central leader should be cut back by removing about half of last summer's new growth, to an upward-pointing bud on the side opposite to last year's leading bud. Laterals, whether they have been summer pruned or not, can be cut back to 7.5cm (3in) for bushes or 5cm (2in) on cordons.

Established gooseberries can be kept in shape through winter pruning, aiming to keep bushes 'cup shaped'. On the main branches the leaders can be cut back by one-third or to fit the space, to an upward-facing bud. An upward-facing bud is selected so that the new growth goes upwards and keeps the leaves and fruit off the ground. Any branches that are damaged, diseased, crossing over or simply in the wrong place should be pruned out in the winter. Lateral shoots growing horizontally from the main branches are cut to about 7.5cm (3in); vertical shoots are best removed back to the main branch, as they will overcrowd the bush once they start to grow, creating an environment that encourages gooseberry sawfly and mildew.

This can be done any time after the leaves have fallen and the plant is dormant, say November, until

Winter pruning gooseberries for shape.

growth starts again in March. Because the fruit buds can be damaged by birds during the winter months as they search for aphids, it may be better to delay winter pruning on these plants until the middle of February, or even the beginning of March, depending on weather conditions. Birds will tend to attack the buds towards the ends of the branches and laterals. By delaying winter pruning any damage can be seen and pruned back to just above sound buds that will

produce fruit. If the pruning is done too early and the birds are hungry, you could potentially lose all the buds you have left.

Gooseberries can be summer pruned from mid-June by cutting new growth back to five leaves, about 7.5cm (3in) from the main branches. This should enable the sun to ripen the fruit and also allows the air to circulate more, helping to reduce the likelihood of American gooseberry mildew getting a hold. It will also remove any growing tips that have already been attacked by mildew. Do not prune the leaders of main branches or cordons in the summer.

Pests, Diseases and Problems

Gooseberries can suffer from problems that affect all fruit, but there are a number of pests and diseases that are specific to gooseberries. Listed below are common problems; please refer to the Pests, Diseases and Problems section within Chapter 4.

American gooseberry mildew
Aphids
Birds and beasts
Coral spot
Dieback
Drought
Frost
Gooseberry sawfly
Honey fungus
Phytophthora
Potash deficiency
Vine weevil

Recommended Varieties

There are hundreds of varieties of gooseberry – you can choose green, yellow, red or white fruits; large, medium or small fruits; round or oval shape, hairy or smooth-skinned. The widest choice will be found in specialist nurseries, and in practice most garden centres only stock two or three popular types, but it is worth tracking down some of the more interesting varieties to bring something unusual and interesting to your garden.

Green

Greenfinch (AGM): some resistance to American gooseberry mildew; produces medium-sized bright green fruit. Season: mid.

Langley Gage: medium to large fruits with superb flavour, as rich and sweet as grapes; some resistance to American gooseberry mildew. Season: mid.

Yellow

Early Sulphur: medium-sized, early season ripening; good flavour if left to ripen as a dessert fruit. Season: early.

Leveller: large yellow fruits with excellent flavour. Season: mid.

ABOVE: **Gooseberry** *Hinnonmaki Red*.

BELOW: **Gooseberry** *Careless*.

Gooseberry *Early Sulphur*.

Red

Hinnonmaki Red (Hinnonmaeki Red): medium-sized fruits, can be picked and cooked as they start to turn pink, but if left to hang the fruits will turn a dark purple-red with a deep, rich flavour; some resistance to American gooseberry mildew. Season: late.

Lancashire Lad: an old variety dating from 1824; thinnings may be green, but if left to hang and ripen they will produce huge tasty red dessert fruits. Season: mid to late to ripen fully.

White

Careless (AGM): produces a prolific quantity of large, pale green fruit; a good 'cooking gooseberry' that will provide enough to eat and plenty to give away. Season: mid.

Invicta (AGM): a sure-fire winner for fruit, and easy to grow as it has some resistance to American gooseberry mildew. Season: mid.

White Eagle: an old variety producing medium to large, well flavoured berries. Season: mid to late.

Raspberry (*Rubus idaeus*)

Who can resist a bowl of summer-fruiting raspberries?

The raspberry is the quintessential summer fruit, much more so than the strawberry, which seems to be available at all times of the year. With their aromatic scent and subtle flavour, a bowl of fresh raspberries needs no further accompaniment. Raspberries are lovely eaten fresh, straight off the cane, and they mix well with other summer fruits, adding a distinctive taste to fruit salads. They make glorious jam and are the basis of genuine Melba sauce. They also freeze and thaw well, which means that the taste of summer can be relived at any time, even in the depths of winter. In the shops they are very expensive, which means that a row of raspberries is one of the most cost-effective fruits that can be grown. They are not always the easiest fruits to grow, but in a good year a row in the right place with the right conditions will provide enough to eat and some to give away to friends and family.

Commercially, raspberry growing is big business, and amateur growers benefit from the research and development that the industry puts into raspberries. There is a continuous programme of raspberry breeding in Britain, which means that new varieties with enhanced flavour and improved resistance to disease and pests seem to appear in nurseries and garden centres just about every season. This presents a dilemma about choosing which raspberry to grow – one of the older, tried and tested varieties, or one of the new and improved varieties. It is worth trying to taste a range of different raspberries, and then choose to grow the one (or ones) you like best.

There are two distinct types of raspberry – the traditional summer-fruiting kind, known as *floricane* varieties, which produce fruit from June through to August on canes that have grown in the previous year, and autumn-fruiting raspberries, *primocane* varieties, which produce fruit from July through to October on canes that have grown from the spring of the current year. Although the growing and cultivation habits are quite different, there is little difference between these two types in terms of flavour, but by choosing carefully you could be picking fresh raspberries for as long as five months.

Always buy plants from reputable garden centres and growers; the plants should be certified as disease- and virus-free.

Planting

Raspberries are usually sold in bundles of individual plants, known as canes, which look like short, 30cm (12in) dry sticks, with a few roots at the end, in a single pot of compost or wrapped in a polythene bag. Planting is best carried out in November, when the soil will still have some residual warmth from the autumn, but they can be planted at any time during the winter when the ground is not frozen or waterlogged. Often bundles of canes are not readily available until late winter. This makes spring planting more likely.

Raspberry canes should be planted out in a prepared site, in a row, spaced about 48cm (15in) apart; if more than one row is planted, they should be spaced about 1.8m (6ft) apart. Do not plant the canes too deep, just

5–7.5cm (2–3in) below the surface. Firm in, water, then mulch with compost to help keep the roots damp as they get established, taking care to prevent the mulch from touching the canes themselves, as this could lead to a fungal infection. Finally, trim all the canes back to about the same length, cutting to just above a bud at about 30cm (12in) above soil level. Raspberry canes planted too deep or cut too low will struggle to get established.

Raspberries need plenty of sun to ripen fully and develop their flavour, but will grow well with some shade, as long as they do not dry out. Try to choose a sheltered site where the plants will not be exposed to cold winds that can damage young new growth. Raspberries do not grow well in heavy soils that stay wet over the winter. If this is your situation, the soil can be improved by digging a trench about 45cm (18in) deep and incorporating plenty of organic matter into the soil when it is backfilled; build up this prepared area so that it is slightly higher, say 7.5–10cm (3–4in) above the surrounding ground; plant into this raised ridge, but still apply a mulch.

Training

Before planting raspberries, it is advisable to prepare the site by deciding how and where they will be trained and supported. Raspberry canes are long and thin, and need to be supported as they grow to help reduce overcrowding and avoid them being blown about in the wind and damaged.

Floricane summer-fruiting raspberries produce fruit on canes that have grown during the previous year. This means that at some time of the year the support you use will need to accommodate not just last year's canes, now fruiting, but also the new growing canes that will produce the fruit next year. Primocane autumn-fruiting raspberries take up less space as there is only ever one season's growth to deal with.

If possible, avoid growing raspberries close to a wall or fence, as ripening on the side towards the wall or fence will be difficult. To give the fruit the best chance of ripening, and to make picking easier, they should ideally be grown in a row. This could take the form of a series of support wires, to which the raspberry canes are tied, fixed to strong, upright posts or stakes. The direction in which the wires run, and consequently the direction in which the growing plants face, may be constrained by the shape and direction of the space available. This may mean that the wires have to be run in line with borders, paths or other garden features. However, in an open area, although the wires could

Raspberries trained against wires.

be run east–west to present the full width of the plant to the sun, this will in practice produce a dense shady area behind the growing plant, which will shade other fruit. In general, if fruit is to be planted in rows, it is better to try to run support wires and posts in a north–south direction, and grow the plants in this plane. In this way each side of the plant is in the sun for part of the day, and the shadow cast will be minimized, enabling fruit to be grown in rows that get more or less equal time in the sun. The space between rows will also be important – about 1.8m (6ft) is recommended between rows of raspberries.

Given optimum space, strong posts of about 7.5–10cm (3–4in) square or diameter, by at least 2.4m (8ft) long, should be fixed into the ground vertically. These posts should be buried at least 60cm (2ft), leaving 1.8m (6ft) out of the ground. Depending on the firmness of the soil, the posts may need to be set in concrete or compacted stones and rubble, or braced with shorter posts angled from the ground to a point at about half the height of the main posts. The posts need to be fixed securely, as once the plant is trained on the wires stretched between them, there will be quite a large area of leaf that will act like a sail as the wind blows, putting great pressure on the wires and posts. To train the plants, galvanized wire of 1.6mm diameter (16 gauge) should be fixed between the main posts, 30cm (12in) apart, starting from about 60cm (24in) up from the ground. Fix the top wire at a height that will be convenient for picking, probably 1.8m (6ft) above ground level. The wire should be stretched, tensioned and fixed firmly, as it will be under great strain when supporting large raspberry plants laden with fruit.

Once the raspberry canes start growing, they can be tied to the wires for support. For floricane summer-fruiting varieties, the new canes that will provide next year's fruit are also tied in as they grow, between last year's fruiting canes, which will be removed once fruiting is over. Try to keep the canes spread out so that there is some air circulation around the fruit to help reduce the chance of mildew. The main thing is to make sure that the new growth each year on summer-fruiting varieties can be identified and kept out of the way of the old canes. Once fruiting has finished, the old canes are removed at ground level, leaving space for the new canes to be tied in.

An alternative to using single wires between posts is the parallel wire system. Here, each row of raspberry canes is sandwiched between two sets of posts and wires, set about 60cm (2ft) apart. The canes are trained between these wires, supported when necessary, but in a much looser way than the single wire system. This allows the new canes to grow up the middle of the row and out of the way of the fruiting canes. However, because the canes are looser, this system is less suitable for windy areas.

If you are growing only a few raspberries, they can be planted and grown in a less formal way, such as a single pillar, supporting the raspberries with garden string tied to bamboo canes or to a single post.

Even unruly raspberries can be grown in containers.

Growing raspberries in large containers has become popular in recent years, and is a system that has been adopted by some pick-your-own farms. Container growing is particularly suitable for primocane autumn-fruiting raspberries as they fruit on the new canes grown each season, so there are fewer canes to deal with. The container should be relatively large, 40–50cm (16–20in) across the top, 50 litres or more, to allow for the development of the canes and sufficient watering. For the planting medium, use a mixture of 80 per cent peat-free multi-purpose compost, ericaceous for preference, plus 20 per cent loam-based potting compost, such as John Innes No. 2; add some grit to aid drainage. Make sure the container is kept watered but not waterlogged; use rainwater if available, as this will help keep the compost slightly acid, which is beneficial for raspberries. Fruit in containers will need feeding more than fruit in the ground, as the nutrients will wash out through the container as it is watered, so add a slow-release fertilizer when mixing the compost, and water regularly with a high potash tomato fertilizer as soon as the fruits are set. Support the growing and fruiting raspberries with garden string tied to a bamboo cane in the centre of the container, or with garden string tied round a series of bamboo canes pushed in around the edge of the container.

Look out for vine weevil infestation in the container – signs include weak growth that does not respond to watering, small white grubs in the compost, and adult vine weevils crawling about on the plants after dark. Hand select and dispose of grubs and adults, and treat containers with a vine weevil nematode if a problem is suspected.

Cultivation

The cultivation of floricane summer-fruiting raspberries is based on looking after and tending the new canes as they grow each year, and removing the old canes after the fruit has been picked, making room for the new canes which will fruit next year.

Cultivation of primocane autumn-fruiting varieties is based on cutting down the old canes that fruited last year in late winter, and encouraging new canes

to grow through the spring and early summer to produce this year's fruit crop.

Raspberries will benefit from mulching in the spring to keep the root area moist; water in dry conditions to help maintain strong, healthy new growth and nice juicy fruit. They will also benefit from a general purpose fertilizer in the spring, and feeding with high potash fertilizer once the fruit has set.

As the plants age, they may start to show signs of fungal or virus problems. These can be managed to some degree, but once they become unhealthy and unproductive it is best to dig them up and dispose of them. It is good practice to replace cane fruit with new, healthy stock every ten years or so, planting in a different part of the garden to reduce the chance of any infection being transferred to the new plants. If there is no opportunity for resiting the cane fruit, the soil around the roots should be replaced with new, fresh soil that is less likely to contain fungal spores that can cause problems.

Raspberries are notoriously difficult to keep in neat rows; they have a habit of producing suckers, or new canes, that spring up at some distance from the original row of plants. If required, these suckers can be used for propagation: dig them up and replant to increase your stock of raspberries, and they should fruit like the parent plant. However, over time there may be some deterioration in the quality of fruit from suckers, as the inevitable virus disease takes hold. If the suckers are not wanted for propagation, just hoe off the tops as they emerge, or if they are too big for this, pull them up and dispose of them.

Like blackcurrants, raspberries need a period of winter chill to allow the plants to rest and gather strength for the next crop. After mild winters crops may be disappointing.

Pruning

Newly planted raspberry canes will not generally require any pruning beyond trimming to a bud about 30cm (12in) above soil level.

Once established and growing, the pruning of floricane summer-fruiting raspberries consists of just cutting and removing the old canes at ground level after the fruit has been picked, making room for the new canes that will fruit next year. Any weak or damaged canes can be removed in the spring. The tips of these canes can be removed if they are too long and cannot be tied into the available wires or framework of supports, or if they have been damaged during the winter. Any further pruning done in the spring should be avoided as this will remove the canes that should be producing the crop of fruit.

Autumn-fruiting raspberries (primocane varieties that fruited last year) should be cut down to ground level in late winter, to encourage new canes to grow through the spring and early summer to produce this year's fruit crop.

When cutting out old canes try not to leave any stubs, or short ends of old canes above the ground, as these will harden and might damage new growth that brushes against them; they are also a potential site for fungal problems.

Pests, Diseases and Problems

Raspberries can suffer from problems that affect all fruit, but there are a number of pests and diseases that are specific to raspberries. Listed below are common problems; please refer to the Pests, Diseases and Problems section within Chapter 4.

Aphids
Birds and beasts
Drought
Frost
Fungal diseases (Cane blight, Cane spot, Purple blotch, Spur blight)
Grey mould
Phytophthora
Raspberry beetle
Vine weevil
Virus disease

Recommended Varieties

With such a wide range of different varieties of raspberry to choose from, the best general advice is to buy certified stock from a reputable supplier; pick a variety that tastes good, grows well and offers some degree of resistance to the problems that can affect cane fruit. Any variety named 'Glen ...' will have been developed by the Scottish Crop Research Institute (SCRI) at Invergowrie; varieties starting with 'Malling ...' will have been developed at East Malling Research (EMR) in Kent.

Summer-fruiting (Floricane)

Glen Ample (AGM): large fruit, excellent flavour, ideal for freezing as fruit does not break up during the process; some resistance to aphids, and tolerance to Phytophthora root rot. Season: mid.

Glen Doll: a useful variety to extend the season of floricane summer-fruiting raspberries; excellent flavour and quality; some resistance to aphids. Season: mid to late.

Glen Moy (AGM): good flavour, fruit of medium size; some resistance to both spur blight and aphids. Season: early.

Glen Prosen (AGM); good crops of medium-sized firm fruit, even in wetter areas. Season: mid.

Julia: canes give high yields of good-sized fruit; some resistance to cane blight, grey mould and other diseases; a good variety for organic growers. Season: mid.

Leo (AGM): large, firm fruit, said to be a good choice for jam-making as the fruit keeps its shape during cooking; some resistance to spur blight. Season: late.

Malling Admiral (AGM): large, tasty fruit, good cropper; grows well in wet areas; some resistance to spur blight. Season: mid to late.

Malling Jewel (AGM): very good flavour. Does not like dry conditions; tolerant of virus infection. Season: early to mid.

Raspberry *Himbo Top*.

Autumn-fruiting (Primocane)

Autumn Bliss (AGM): combines the best of all raspberry characteristics; good-sized crops of large fruits of excellent flavour, easy pruning in late winter, fruiting on current season's new growth; some resistance to aphids and Phytophthora root rot. Season: successional picking from July to October.

All Gold: golden yellow fruit, yet with a good raspberry flavour, sweet. Season: August to September.

Himbo Top: a relatively new variety, bred in Switzerland; produces large succulent fruit that seem to hold their shape better in damp autumn conditions. Season: mid-August to October.

Raspberry *All Gold*.

Redcurrants (*Ribes rubrum*) and White Currants (*Ribes vulgare*)

Jewel-like redcurrants make an attractive fruit in any garden.

Redcurrants can be the most attractive fruit in the garden, hanging in long strigs, glistening like jewels as the summer sun shines through the clear red fruit. White currants are a pale, translucent form of the same fruit, but no less attractive. Even more attractive, and certainly unusual, are the pink currants that can sometimes be found in old gardens, or from specialist nurseries.

Ripe redcurrants are sweet and juicy, and can be eaten raw straight off the plant; they can be mixed with other summer fruit to form a luscious mixed fruit salad, or cooked into tasty pies and tarts. Picked before they are ripe, they will be sharp, and ideal for savoury sauces, but they may need sugar if used for desserts. If left to hang, redcurrants will continue ripening and become sweeter all the while the summer sun shines. Left too long, however, the quality of the fruit will start to decline.

The information and guidance given for redcurrants will apply equally to white currants and pink currants, the only difference being that redcurrant plants tend to be more vigorous than white currants, and the fruit is usually larger than that of most varieties of white currant.

Planting

Redcurrants are related to gooseberries and will certainly produce fruit even if grown in some shade, but full sun will make sure that the redcurrants colour up, ripen and develop their distinct flavour.

When planting new redcurrants, the soil should be kept at the same level as it was in the nursery or container. The same applies to bare-rooted plants – keep the soil at the same level that the plant was at in the nursery.

Newly planted redcurrants will benefit from being given support; the simplest way is to tie them to a cane inserted into the ground about 7.5cm (3in) from the plant, avoiding its roots if possible. If there is a row of cordon redcurrants, the canes can be tied to wires for additional support.

Redcurrants can be successfully grown in containers; make sure the roots have sufficient room and that the container is kept watered, but not waterlogged. For best results use a soil-based potting compost with some grit added to improve drainage. Fruit in containers will need feeding more than fruit in the ground, as the nutrients will wash out through the container as it is watered.

Look out for vine weevil infestation in the container – signs include weak growth that does not respond to watering, small white grubs in the compost, and adult vine weevils crawling about on the plants after dark. Hand select and dispose of grubs and adults, and treat containers with a vine weevil nematode if a problem is suspected.

Training

As with gooseberries, there are a number of ways to grow redcurrants; pick the one that suits the available space or the shape that you prefer.

Bush: this is the traditional shape, and is likely to be the basic form in which you buy a new redcurrant plant from a garden centre or nursery. It will make cultivation easier if the bush is grown on a single leg, a length of bare plant between the ground and where the branches start, about 25–30cm (10–12in) above ground level. This is to provide air flow under the bush, and will help to make sure that branches laden with fruit do not drag on the ground and get dirty from rain splash or eaten by slugs and the like. Having space below the branches will also make picking easier, and the glorious fruit will hang down like jewels.

Viewed from above, a redcurrant bush should have four or five main horizontal branches radiating out from the main stem. It is good practice to try to prune a bush-grown redcurrant into an 'open cup' shape. This means cutting out any vertical growth from the centre of the bush, but leaving new growth around the outer circumference.

Plant bush-grown redcurrant bushes about 1.5m (5ft) apart; allow about 1.5m (5ft) between rows.

Standard: this means growing the bush shape high up off the ground. The bush is simply lifted from ground level up a long straight leg that can be 90cm–1.2m (3–4ft) high to a height which allows the fruit to be picked without the need to bend down. A standard redcurrant can also be an attractive and unusual talking point. Standard redcurrants can sometimes be bought ready trained from nurseries and garden centres. You can grow your own standard redcurrant from a cutting or a single cordon plant by removing all side shoots and allowing the central leader to continue growing upwards. When it reaches beyond the required height, prune it back in the winter at the desired height to a strong, upward-facing bud. The new growth in the spring should start to produce branches that can be shaped, as described, for a bush. A standard-grown redcurrant will need to be supported throughout its life by a sturdy stake or strong cane, as a leafy bush at the top of a single leg can become heavy and become damaged, especially in heavy rain or strong winds.

Cordon: cordon growing is ideal for redcurrants as it provides good air flow and makes fruit picking easy as the fruit hangs from short lateral spurs. A cordon is essentially a straight main branch growing vertically, tied to a cane or horizontal wires for support. A single cordon can be developed by allowing the central leader of a new cutting to continue growing upward, keeping the lateral side shoots pruned to a bud at about 2.5cm (1in) in the winter, brutting new growth to about half its length or 10cm (4in) in the summer. Double or triple cordons can be developed by allowing a second or third vertical branch to grow up from about 15cm (6in) above soil level. Hard pruning the leader of a single cordon to upward-facing buds at about this height in the winter will encourage strong new shoots in the spring, the strongest of which

Cordon redcurrants can produce a lot of fruit in a small space.

can be selected and trained up as vertical cordons. Unwanted shoots can be stopped by pruning them and rubbing off any subsequent buds that form.

Plant single redcurrant cordons 38–45cm (15–18in) apart, depending on the space available; double cordons will need to be planted about 60cm (24in) apart, to allow each stem of the cordon to be spaced 30cm (12in) apart. Leave 1.2–1.5m (4–5ft) between rows of cordons to allow good air flow. Make sure that each cordon is supported by a cane tied to horizontal wires.

Redcurrants can also be trained in more decorative forms, such as fans, which can be grown to cover a fence panel or wall. The basic principles of fan training are covered in Chapter 1.

Cultivation

Redcurrants and white currants can be planted in the ground or grown in containers. Container-grown plants are available throughout the year and can be planted at more or less any time, but avoid planting once the fruit has set as there is a good chance that it will be lost as the plant goes into shock as a result of the replanting. The best time to buy and plant is when they are dormant, after leaf fall in the autumn and before the new buds open in the early spring. At this stage the shape and form of the plant can be seen clearly and any formative pruning required to shape the plant can be done easily. Planting can take place whenever the ground is accessible and not too wet, from autumn through to spring.

As the fruit of redcurrants and white currants is produced from buds on spurs, on ripe wood and around the base of the previous year's growth, it is winter pruning that is most important for fruit production. This can be done any time after the leaves have fallen and the plant is dormant, say November, until growth starts again in March. It consists of cutting back previously summer-pruned laterals to above buds at about 10cm (2in) if being grown as bushes, or to 2.5cm (1in) on cordons. Because the fruit buds

can be damaged by birds during the winter months as they search for aphids, it is better to delay winter pruning on these plants until the middle of February. The leaders of the main branches of bush-grown plants are cut back by about half of last season's growth to a bud that is pointing upwards and outwards – this will produce new growth that is strong enough to support this year's fruit crop. On cordons, the leaders are cut back by up to half of the previous season's new growth, to an upward-pointing bud, to continue to encourage strong vertical growth. Once a cordon has reached the desired height, up to about 1.5–1.8m (5–6ft), cut back each winter to a bud at about this height. By pruning later in the winter, any damaged or crossing branches can be seen and removed by cutting back to sound and healthy wood. Look out for branches that have died back and are host to coral spot fungus – remove them by cutting back to healthy wood.

Flowering tends to be relatively early, especially if there are any unseasonably warm days, and bushes should be protected with horticultural fleece if frost is forecast. The flowers are borne in long strigs hanging down from the branch or fruiting spur, and they tend

Redcurrants in flower.

to open closest to the branch first, progressing down to the end of the strig as the season moves on and the weather gets a bit better. This means that there may be tiny fruit set at the top of the strig while there are flowers opening at the tip – the aim of the fruit grower is to get fruit from the top to the tip of the strig. The flowers are often open on cold days in early spring when there are few insects about. Pollination levels can be improved if there is a good air flow round the plants. Lightly tapping the branches when the flowers are open fully and the pollen is ripe helps to shake the pollen into the flowers.

The set fruit will swell quickly if there is sufficient rain; if not, watering may be necessary.

With redcurrants, summer pruning takes the form of 'brutting' – that is snapping off about half the length of the new season's growth on the laterals, across the blunt back of a pruning knife, or across the unopened blades of secateurs. The action of snapping, rather than cutting, seems to prevent any regrowth and nutrients that would otherwise go to leaf production instead go to help the fruit to swell. The removal of the leafy new growth allows more sun to reach the currants and improves ripening. Any damage from gooseberry sawfly should also be removed.

Established redcurrants benefit from a light sprinkling of a general purpose fertilizer that has a good balance of nutrients and trace elements in the very early spring. This is also a good time to apply sulphate

of potash if required – alternatively, apply a sprinkling of wood ash over the area of the roots, which can be produced by burning the wood removed during winter pruning. Avoid fertilizers with high levels of nitrogen, as this can encourage soft growth which tends to be more susceptible to aphid attack. Once the fruit has set, a tomato fertilizer that is high in potash can be applied to help the fruit develop. A mulch of compost in the spring will help retain the moisture in the soil surrounding the plants. Be careful when applying the mulch to avoid touching the leg of the plant with the compost. Keeping it clean by brushing the compost away will help prevent soil-based fungal infections, such as *Phytophthora*, from attacking the plant.

Redcurrant plants will produce fruit within their first year, although it is advisable to remove these to encourage the development of a stronger root system. Fruiting will be at its best after three or four years. The plants will live for over twenty years or more, but fruit production will decline unless new, replacement growth is encouraged through winter pruning,

After brutting, half of the new season's growth has been removed.

Brutting redcurrants in the summer.

Redcurrant before winter pruning showing laterals growing from the main branch.

cutting out old, less productive branches or cordons. This treatment may become necessary as old cordons sometimes die back completely.

Propagation can be done by taking hard-wood cuttings in the autumn.

Pruning

Newly planted redcurrants will require some initial formative pruning to remove any crossing or damaged branches and to start to get the plant to grow into the required shape. For bush training, four or five well-spaced leaders radiating out from the leg should be selected and shortened by half, to an upward- and outward-pointing bud. Aim to produce a cup shape, with an open centre to the bush. Remove branches that are in the wrong place, cutting right back to the leg on which the bush will grow. Weak laterals can

be removed, and the laterals that remain should be trimmed to a bud about 7.5cm (3in) out from the branch. If the new plant is to be trained as a cordon, the plant needs to be encouraged to put its energies into a single, strong, upright growth. Select the strongest upright growth coming from the centre of the plant and cut all other branches back to within 7.5cm (3in) of what will become the central leader; prune this leader back, by up to half the length of the new growth that was made during the previous season, to an upward-pointing bud that will produce strong new growth.

Redcurrants produce fruit buds on spurs, on ripe wood and around the base of the previous year's growth, so the aim of winter pruning is to produce a strong spur system on laterals on the main branches; cutting back the leaders of the main branches by about half of last season's growth to a bud that is

After pruning, the laterals have been pruned back to one bud.

pointing upwards and outwards will help stimulate the growth of strong branches and laterals. If the plant is being trained as a cordon, the central leader should be cut back by about half of last summer's new growth, to an upward-pointing bud on the side opposite to last year's leading bud. Laterals, whether they have been summer pruned or not, can be cut back to buds at 5cm (2in) for bushes or about 2.5cm (1in) on cordons.

Established redcurrants can be kept in shape through winter pruning. Aim to keep bushes 'cup shaped' – that is, with an open centre, with four or five main branches radiating out from the centre of the bush. The main branches, the leaders, can be cut back by one-third or to fit the space, to an upward-facing bud. An upward-facing bud is selected so that the new growth goes upwards and keeps the leaves and fruit off the ground. Any branches that are damaged, diseased, crossing over or simply in the wrong place should be pruned out in the winter. Lateral shoots growing horizontally from the main branches are cut to about 7.5cm (3in); vertical shoots are best removed back to the main branch, as they will overcrowd the bush once they start to grow, creating an environment that encourages gooseberry sawfly and mildew.

White currants can be treated in the same way as redcurrants, but as they tend to be less vigorous, producing new growth that is shorter, it may be better to summer prune them in the same way as gooseberries.

Pests, Diseases and Problems

Redcurrants can suffer from problems that affect all fruit, but there are a number of pests and diseases that are specific to redcurrants. Listed below are common problems; please refer to the Pests, Diseases and Problems section within Chapter 4.

Aphids
Birds and beasts
Coral spot
Currant clearwing moth
Dieback
Drought
Frost
Gooseberry sawfly
Honey fungus
Phytophthora
Potash deficiency
Vine weevil

Recommended Varieties
Redcurrants

Jonkheer van Tets (AGM): produces huge fruit with a good flavour; if left to ripen will develop a particularly deep red. Season: early.

Redcurrant *Jonkheer van Tets*.

Red Lake (AGM): this used to be a commercial variety, and as such is extremely prolific; a good general purpose redcurrant. Season: mid to late.

Redcurrant *Wilsons Long Bunch*.

Rovada: usually produces heavy crops of large fruit with a good flavour, on long strigs. Season: late.

Wilson's Long Bunch: one of the best tasting redcurrants; crimson fruit hangs on exceptionally long strigs. Season: late.

White Currants

White Dutch: an extremely old variety; good flavour when ripe, and usually larger fruit than White Versailles. Season: mid.

White Versailles: this is the variety that is most readily available in garden centres. If left to ripen the fruits will be very sweet and tasty, but they tend to be smaller and produce a lower weight of fruit per plant than similar-sized redcurrant bushes. Season: early to mid.

White currant *White Versailles*.

Strawberry (*Fragaria*)

The strawberry – everyone's summer favourite.

The strawberry is a favourite fruit for many people, and its popularity has meant that supermarket strawberries are available virtually all year round as the result of retailers and growers around the world working together to develop varieties that will ensure continuity of supply and fruit that reaches the customer in good condition. So why bother to grow your own? There has been a price to pay for the convenience of year-round strawberries: the joy and anticipation of the coming strawberry season has gone, and it has been noticed that, although strawberries may have got bigger and redder, they have lost some of the magic strawberry aroma and perhaps are not quite as tasty as they used to be; even the texture of some supermarket strawberries is different: firm and almost crunchy.

But all is not lost. The strawberry is a relatively easy fruit to grow: it is self-fertile, does not need pruning, and as long as it is fed and watered (and protected from pests) you can be sure of a crop. Strawberry plants are relatively small and self-contained, so you can grow as many or as few as can fit into the space available. And as far as flavour is concerned, there is nothing quite like the taste of fresh strawberries picked straight off the plant.

There are three main types of strawberry that you can grow:

Summer-fruiting: the classic, large-fruiting strawberry varieties that flower in the late spring and produce one crop of fruit during the summer. Their normal strawberry season is June and July, depending on the variety grown; some varieties may have a second flush of flowers that will fruit during the autumn. However, by careful selection of varieties, the use of chilled runners, and skilled plant management, strawberries can be produced almost to order, sixty to ninety days after planting.

Large-fruited, perpetual, everbearers: these flower later, during the summer months, but will produce fruit over a few months, from mid-summer through into the autumn.

Alpine: also perpetual, these are like wild strawberries; they are small plants, producing masses of tiny but extremely tasty fruit through the summer.

Planting and Cultivation

There has been something of a revolution in the way that strawberries are planted and grown, with the realization that, although the classic and traditional approach of planting in the open garden is still valid and effective, there are many more novel ways of planting and growing strawberries, which can make life easier for the gardener and increase the chances of producing a good crop.

Small, new-season strawberry plants are available in garden centres from the middle of the summer. The sooner they are planted the better, so that they can get established and build up energy reserves and flower buds to produce a crop the following year. The later planting is delayed, the smaller the crop the following year. If planting occurs after autumn or in the spring, it will help the plant to get established if any flowers that are produced in that first season are removed so that fruiting is delayed for a year – this will result in a stronger plant and ultimately a much bigger crop the next year. But it takes a strong will to resist letting the plants produce fruit for a year, and you may decide that a small crop now is better than waiting for a marginally bigger crop in the future.

Cold-stored strawberry plants, available from some suppliers, can be planted from March to July, and these will grow, flower and produce a satisfactory crop from sixty to ninety days after planting.

Always buy plants from reputable garden centres and growers; the plants should be certified as disease- and virus-free.

Ground Planting

Strawberries like a soil that is rich in nutrients, has a lot of organic matter dug into it, and yet drains well. If you are starting with a fresh piece of ground, it will need to be cleared of all perennial weeds, dug over, and enriched with compost or organic matter a few weeks before planting takes place. A dressing of general purpose fertilizer will also help, as a strawberry bed could remain productive for a number of years. Once the soil has settled, remove any leaves or organic matter that could harbour slugs. Plant in blocks or rows, allowing 30–46cm (12–18in) between plants, and 60–75cm (24–30in) between rows, depending on space. The crown of the plant should be at soil level, neither too deep nor standing proud of the soil. Water in, and try not to let the ground dry out as the plants become established. The water should be directed straight into the ground around the plants, trying not to wet the developing flowers, as this could encourage the development of Botrytis (grey mould) on the fruit. Keep the ground between plants clear as they grow, weeding either by hand or with a hoe. Weeds will take moisture and nutrients from the soil and provide a hiding-place for slugs.

Once the flowers open and are pollinated the fruit will start to develop. Maintain watering at this stage to help the fruit to swell, adding a dilute high potash tomato fertilizer once a week to help improve the fruit quality. As the fruit gets heavier the trusses will need to be supported to prevent the fruit touching the ground, where it will get dirty and be readily available for damage from slugs. The traditional solution is to gently lift up the fruiting truss and put a layer of straw underneath, before resting the fruit on it. Straw will keep the fruit clean, dry, and up and away from slugs.

Strawberry plant in flower.

Purpose-made strawberry mats are also available in garden centres as a modern and tidier alternative to straw.

As soon as the strawberries start to colour, cover the plants with a net to protect the crop from hungry birds.

Keep picking the fruit as required; do not leave it to get wet or to hang too long as this will encourage Botrytis (grey mould). Remove and dispose of any mouldy or damaged fruits to help preserve those that are left on the plant.

As soon as fruiting has finished, cut off the old leaves 10cm (4in) or so above the crown, trying not to damage the new leaves which are developing. This allows light to reach the crown and stimulates the development of flower buds for the next season.

Clear the area around the strawberries by removing the straw, any weeds and any loose leaves. This will help reduce the chance of pests and disease lingering around the plants. Boost the plants with a light top-dressing of sulphate of potash, which will help them recover and get ready for the next year.

After fruiting, each plant will start to throw off long thin 'runners'; at the tip of each runner will be an embryo strawberry plant. If more plants are required, these runners can be pegged down into the ground or into 10cm (4in) pots of compost. The tip will quickly take root and develop into a new plant, which can be detached from the main plant once it has become

Strawberry runner ready for propagation.

established. Allow no more than one or two good runners from each plant; remove all the others as they will tend to weaken the plant and reduce the crop next year. If no more strawberry plants are required, cut off all the runners at their base as soon as they emerge from the crown of the main plant.

Propagating from runners is a good way of increasing the stock of strawberry plants, but over time the health of the runners may start to deteriorate as diseases and viruses start to weaken the plants. There will come a point when you need to completely restock with new plants that are certified disease- and virus-free.

Keeping strawberry plants healthy and cropping to their full potential is important. Commercial growers achieve this by treating their strawberry plants as annuals, but this is somewhat wasteful for garden growing. A good way for the garden fruit grower is to establish a cycle of planting, propagating new plants and discarding old plants over a period of three or four years. The quantity and quality of fruit from a strawberry plant will peak in years two and three, and start to decline thereafter, so it is important to keep a supply of new plants coming to replace the old plants. This system takes up a lot of garden space, and is probably easier to manage if the strawberries are planted in growing bags or containers.

A variation on planting straight into the ground is to plant through a sheet of black polythene laid over the ground. Raise slight ridges, 7.5cm (3in) high, in the soil where the strawberries are to be planted, and cover these with the polythene; in this way, rain will drain into the soil between the plants rather than pooling round the crown and rotting the plant. Once the ground is prepared, the polythene is fixed down with bricks or pegs, and slits cut in the polythene along the ridges where the plants are to be positioned; the strawberry roots go through the polythene and are planted into the ground below, while the leaves remain sticking out of the polythene. The soil should be damp before the polythene is fixed down. Leave a strip of bare soil between the plants or rows, so that excess water will drain into the soil and feed the plants. There are a number of reasons why some growers do this: the polythene suppresses weeds, it acts as a mulch, reducing moisture loss from the ground and thus helping the fruit to develop and swell, and it helps to keep the fruit clean, as soil will not splash on to the fruit during watering or when it rains. There are, however, risks from this method of growing: it can be more difficult to monitor watering, unless you are very careful to make sure that each plant is watered individually through the polythene, and there is a risk that the polythene sheet will act as a safe haven for slugs. Horticultural polythene is available; alternatively, use large compost bags that are often black on the inside. Slit these down the sides and lay printed side down.

Strawberries in Growing Bags

The growing bag, filled with fresh, rich compost, has become an important and versatile way of extending the range of plants grown in many gardens. For the strawberry grower, the growing bag has a number of attractions and advantages over ground planting. A new growing bag guarantees a consistent quality of sterile compost, so there is no concern over soil-borne disease; watering and feeding can be finely controlled and optimized to suit conditions; and with the possibility of squeezing up to six strawberry plants

Strawberries in growing bags well protected from birds by netting.

into one growing bag, it makes very good use of the space available.

Developing a bag rotation cycle is easy, starting new bags each year and disposing of the oldest, to maximize fruit production – make sure each bag is dated, so you know which is the oldest and is therefore due for replacement as it reaches the end of its three years of fruiting. The relatively small size of a growing bag means that it is easy to net to protect the fruit from birds.

But perhaps the greatest advantage of a growing bag for strawberries is its portability, which means that it can be lifted up off the ground and placed in a sunny area on an outdoor bench or shelving system. This lifts the plants up and away from soil and slug problems; watering and tending can be done without the need to bend down; the fruit will be clean, and the trusses of fruit hang down for easy picking. If you want more strawberries just plant up more growing bags: it is as simple as that. Cultivation of strawberries in growing bags is basically the same as for ground planting: keep the crown of the plant level with the compost, keep the bag well watered, but not waterlogged, feed with a high potash tomato fertilizer as soon as the fruit is set, pick and enjoy, remove old leaves and unwanted runners after fruiting to allow light to reach the crown and stimulate the development of flower buds for the next season. Water in a soluble general fertilizer each spring to give the plants a boost for the season, and maintain feeding with a high potash tomato fertilizer when in fruit.

There are a number of purpose-built strawberry growing systems available, based on the use of a growing bag as the planting medium, which incorporate irrigation and a framework for netting to protect the crop.

Container Growing

For strawberry growers, the choice of containers is limited only by the imagination. There are traditional strawberry planters – basically a large pot with holes or moulded pockets around the sides, filled with compost, into which strawberry runners are inserted; garden centres also offer a range of towers, patio planters and pot systems for growing strawberries. They can be planted as a decorative and edible edge to large tubs or containers housing flowers or shrubs. Whichever style of container you choose, try to keep to the basic requirements for strawberries: good-quality compost, regular watering and feeding, and protection from slugs and birds.

Strawberries plants grown in terracotta pots.

An intensive yet productive form of container growing is based on planting individual strawberry plants into 2-litre pots. Use a good-quality compost – mix up 50 per cent loam-based compost, such as John Innes no. 2, with 50 per cent peat-free multi-purpose, plus some grit for drainage, and add a little slow-release fertilizer. Pot up runners in late summer or early spring each year. Keep the plants watered and feed with a high potash tomato fertilizer once a week as soon as the first fruit has set. Fill as many or as few pots as there is space. Place in a sunny area, out of reach of slugs, and protect from birds. Pick and enjoy fruit as it develops. Remove old leaves and unwanted runners after fruiting; this allows light to reach the crown and stimulates the development of flower buds for the next season. Top-dress each pot each spring with a little fresh compost and a pelleted general fertilizer, or water in a soluble general fertilizer. By potting up a few new runners each year you can start to build up a bank of potted strawberry plants that will provide fruit on a cycle of, say, three years; after this time the plants

can be disposed of as the new plants come into maximum cropping. Keeping the plants for no longer than three years means that the plants should stay healthy, and you dispose of any soil-borne pests such as vine weevil grubs. Treat pots with a vine weevil nematode if vine weevil infestation is suspected, evidenced by weak growth in the spring, few roots left in the pot when inspected, and the appearance of white grubs within the compost. Destroy any vine weevil grubs that are found, and do not reuse the compost as it is likely to spread the problem elsewhere in the garden.

Strawberries grown intensively in 2-litre pots.

Make sure that each pot is dated so you know which ones are the oldest and therefore due for replacement as they reach the end of the three years of fruiting.

Look out for vine weevil infestation in the containers – signs include weak growth that does not respond to watering, small white grubs in the compost, and adult vine weevils crawling about on the plants after dark. Hand select and dispose of grubs and adults, and treat containers with a vine weevil nematode if a problem is suspected.

Pests, Diseases and Problems

Strawberries can suffer from problems that affect all fruit, but there are a number of pests and diseases that are specific to strawberries. Listed below are common problems; please refer to the Pests, Diseases and Problems section within Chapter 4.

Aphids
Birds and beasts
Drought
Frost
Grey mould
Phytophthora
Potash deficiency
Powdery mildew
Slug and snails
Verticillium wilt
Vine weevil
Viruses

Recommended Varieties

There are so many varieties available that the main criteria can only be flavour (grow the ones you like the taste of) and space (how much room should you devote to strawberries). The more space you have, of course, the wider the range of strawberries that can be grown. To ensure a strawberry crop over a longer period of time, grow a few plants from a range of different varieties that will crop from early summer through to the autumn. For something really special, grow varieties that are not available in the supermarkets.

Summer-fruiting

Cambridge Late Pine: an old variety with excellent flavour; some resistance to powdery mildew. Season: mid-June to mid-July.

Cambridge Vigour: not widely available, but a really tasty fruit that is worth tracking down. Season: early, June.

Ken Muir's exhibition stand at the RHS Chelsea Flower Show, demonstrating the wide range of strawberries available for the fruit grower.

Honeoye (AGM): heavy cropping, with nicely shaped conical fruit of good flavour. Season: early, June to the start of July.

Rhapsody (AGM): good-sized fruit, good flavour; some resistance to disease and mildew. Season: late, July.

Royal Sovereign: a heritage variety with an 'old-fashioned' strawberry flavour; introduced in 1892, it became the gardeners' favourite through the first half of the twentieth century; virus and disease pushed it to the verge of extinction, but cleaned-up certified stock has become available in recent years. Season: mid-June to early July.

Large-fruited Perpetual Everbearers

Aromel (AGM): good flavour and relatively large fruit, although not many on the plant at any one time. Season: July to October.

Mara des Bois: good-sized fruits which have the taste of wild or alpine strawberries; some resistance to powdery mildew. Season: August to October.

Alpine

Often sold without a varietal name, but some of the better cultivars do have names. Alpine strawberries can be grown from seed sown in late winter/early spring, as well as being available as plants. Season: June to end of October.

Alba: a real novelty, small white fruit, but with the alpine strawberry taste.

Alexandria: fruit somewhat larger than other alpine strawberries, yet retains its distinctive flavour.

Baron Solemache – considered to be one of the original cultivars, selected because of the exquisitely sweet flavour; this variety tends to produce fewer runners than others, and is therefore easier to manage in the garden situation.

Strawberry *Honeoye.*

Tree Fruit

Apple (*Malus domestica*)

A beautiful selection of the 2,000+ varieties of apple that can be grown in this country, on display at the RHS Great Autumn Show.

Apples must be one of the most popular fruits eaten and grown in Britain, being suited to the climate and our culture. Apples are grown from Lands End to Scotland, through Wales and Northern Ireland, and 'an apple a day keeps the doctor away' has been a British mantra for at least a hundred years, with some merit, it has to be said   apples contain Vitamin C, lots of fibre, can help keep teeth free of harmful bacteria, and are claimed to have many other health-giving properties. In addition, with over 2,000 varieties to choose from, there must be an apple to suit most tastes as well as most growing conditions. The year-round availability of apples in our shops, many of them imported, masks the fact that apples are seasonal, like all fruit, but with careful planning and storage home-grown apples can be available from August through to the following March or April. An apple plucked from a tree and eaten, still warm from the sun, is a glorious fruit – the most difficult decision is which of the many varieties to grow.

There may well be apple trees in your garden already, or you may have a favourite that you would like to grow. Whatever the situation, take a moment to think through how to get the best crop and the best quality for your needs and your garden. Once you have decided which varieties of apple you would like to grow, there are several other factors that you need to take into account.

Shape and Size of Tree

While the shape of the tree is (mostly) up to you as the grower, and as the person who prunes and cultivates the tree to whichever shape or form that you want, the size will be influenced by the rootstock on which your chosen variety has been grown.

Apple rootstocks are identified by numbers that bear no relationship to size in absolute terms or in relation to one another. The rootstock numbers were, in fact, allocated in sequence of the order in which they were put into trials to see how the rootstock performed in terms of speed of growth and the ultimate size reached after a number of years. The rootstock will also have a bearing on how long you will have to wait before the tree starts to bear fruit, and on the size and quality of that fruit.

When you buy an apple tree from a nursery, you can specify which rootstock you want; from a garden centre or other type of retail outlet there may not always be a choice, or even an indication of which rootstock you are buying. If in doubt, ask and make sure that it is what you want – if not, shop elsewhere.

Apples on rootstock M26 are probably the most commonly available; it is versatile enough for most forms of training and will produce a reasonable sized tree up to about 2.4m (10ft) on average soils, and should start to produce fruit from its second or third year. If the soil is poor, rootstock MM106 is perhaps a better choice as it is still very versatile but a bit more vigorous.

Most apple trees sold through garden centres and nurseries will be one or two years old and will have already received some formative pruning and training to give them a general tree-like appearance. This is fine if you want to continue with this shape and form of tree, which will eventually grow into a larger version of what you buy, within the natural limitations of its rootstock.

Ready-trained apple trees are often available in three main forms, espalier, fan and stepover, grown on appropriate rootstocks. These will be two or three years old, depending on how much training has been done and the stage that it has reached. Inevitably, these will be more expensive as the nursery will have had to invest time and skill in growing and training the trees into the different forms.

For single cordons, or to do your own training, you will need a maiden tree where pruning and training have not yet started. These can be found in some garden centres, but are more commonly offered by nurseries.

More information about growing forms and training can be found in Chapter 1.

Pollination

Most apples are self-fertile to some degree, but a second tree will be required to improve pollination, increase the fruit set and the quality of the fruit –

unless, of course, there are apple trees growing in neighbouring gardens which can do the job. If you are growing *Bramley's Seedling*, *Jonagold* or another triploid apple, a third tree will be required to complete the pollination as the pollen from triploids will not be effective on other trees. Choose apple trees from the same or adjacent flowering groups to make sure that they are all in flower at more or less the same time. A family tree, with different varieties growing on a single rootstock, is another way of making sure that effective pollination occurs. Another solution is to grow a crab apple, such as *John Downie* or *Golden Hornet*, to ensure good cross-pollination; this has the bonus of fruit for crab apple jelly or wine-making.

The flowering group should be shown clearly on the growers' label attached to the tree when you buy it. If it does not, ask for advice.

Planting

Apple trees are sold either bare-rooted, containerized or container-grown. Decide where the tree is to be planted and dig out a hole big enough to contain the rootball with room to spare. The hole should be deep enough to allow the tree to be planted at the same depth as it was in the nursery or container, so that the soil line around the tree is level with the surrounding soil. The depth and soil level can be checked by laying a garden cane across the top of the hole, resting it on the soil on either side. Incorporate some compost or a small amount of farmyard manure in the bottom of the planting hole, breaking up the soil at the base of the hole if it is hard – this will help the roots get established. Sprinkle the soil that has been removed and will be used to backfill the hole with a long-term, slow-release fertilizer such as blood, fish and bone. Place the new tree into the centre of the hole and spread out the roots. With a container-grown tree, tease out some of the roots gently, without breaking them, so that they are encouraged to grow out and into the surrounding soil, rather than continue growing round and round as they have done in the

John Downie **crab apple flowers are a great pollinator.**

An abundant *Golden Hornet* in autumn, showing off its bright yellow fruits.

container. Support the tree so that it will stay at the right depth, and check the depth against the garden cane laid across the planting hole. Backfill with the soil that has been dug out, firming as you go, and keeping the trunk upright (unless it is being deliberately angled for oblique cordons). Puddling-in can be done when the hole is half-filled, by pouring water into the planting hole; keep the trunk upright and resume backfilling once the water has drained away. Finish the planting by making sure that the tree is level with the surrounding soil. Mulch around the tree, making sure that it does not come into direct contact with the trunk. Water regularly to help the new tree get established. In dry areas it may be useful to raise a ridge of soil in a circle around the new tree, up to 1m (39in) across, to create a saucer-like effect with the tree in the centre; this will help concentrate water in the root area and prevent water running away and being wasted.

Stake securely to support the new tree as it establishes its root system and to reduce wind rock. The stake should be driven at an angle into the ground, avoiding the area of the roots, so that it meets the tree at a point half-way up the trunk at an angle of about 45°; tie the tree to the stake using a soft rubber tree-tie or garden twine. Make sure the tie is not too tight and check it regularly to make sure that it does not restrict the flow of sap as the tree grows; also make sure that the tree and the stake do not rub together as this could damage the bark and provide an entry point for disease.

Once established, apple trees growing in the

ground will not need much feeding; sprinkle a little sulphate of potash over the root area in February, or water in a high potash tomato fertilizer once the fruit has set. An autumn mulch that incorporates a little farmyard manure will give weak-growing trees a boost of nitrogen to help them put on some new growth. Container-grown apples will need to have the top few centimetres of compost renewed each year; because the nutrients will be washed out through regular watering, incorporate a slow-release general fertilizer in the top-dressing. Once the fruit has set, container-grown trees will benefit from a regular feed of high potash tomato fertilizer.

Do not stint on watering during dry periods. New plantings will need regular watering in dry periods to help establish their root structure; trees in fruit will start to drop the fruit if the tree becomes stressed through lack of water.

Cultivation

Apple trees are usually planted in the ground, but on a dwarfing rootstock they will grow and fruit in containers, such as large pots. Container-grown trees are available through the year and can be planted at more or less any time, but avoid planting once the fruit has set as there is a good chance that it will be lost as the plant goes into shock as a result of the replanting. The best time to buy and plant apple trees is when they are dormant, after leaf fall in the autumn and before the new buds open in the early spring. At this stage the shape and form of the plant can be seen clearly and any formative pruning required to shape the plant can be done easily. Planting can be done whenever the ground is accessible and not too wet, from autumn, when the ground is still warm, through to spring.

Different varieties of apple have different habits in the way that the fruit is produced: some apple trees are 'spur bearers', which produce apples on fruiting spurs created in previous seasons; others are 'tip bearers', where the apples grow on the tips of short laterals growing from the main branches. Confusingly, some apples trees will produce fruit on spurs and tips; these are known as 'partial tip bearers'. From the point of

view of choosing varieties that you like to eat and want to grow, these designations may seem somewhat academic, but the way in which they fruit will determine how you need to summer prune for fruit.

Pruning

For most apples and pears, it is best to keep a close watch for the 'terminal buds' that develop on the tips of this year's new growth. Through the spring and early summer the tips of the new growth on apples and pears will be leafy and bright green. Summer pruning at this stage will simply result in more young growth, especially if it is a wet summer. However, the new growth will reach a point when it slows down, and the growing tip starts to change from leaves into a small tight 'terminal bud' – it is at this point that summer pruning should be carried out. This may not happen at the same time over all of the tree, so pruning can be spread over a number of days as and when the terminal buds are just right.

The soft growing tip of new summer growth on an apple before the terminal bud has formed.

If the new growth is a lateral – a new shoot coming straight out from the branch – it can be used to start the formation of a spur that will bear fruit in the future. This is done by cutting back any new lateral that is over 20cm (8in) to three leaves above the cluster of

Terminal bud formed on the end of the current season's growth shows that is ready for summer pruning.

small leaves around the base of the new shoot where it grows out of the branch. If the new growth is from a spur that has been formed in previous years, cut it back to just one leaf up from the cluster of small leaves around the base of the shoot. Any new lateral growth that is shorter than 20cm (8in) can be left unpruned.

This form of summer pruning should work for most apples and pears. However, there are a number of varieties of apple and pear, and all varieties of quince, that produce fruit on the tips of shoots from older wood, and do not form spurs. For these 'tip bearers' concentrate on winter pruning to establish the shape of tree that you require, and in the summer just trim new laterals to 20cm (8in), leaving unpruned any that are shorter than this.

There is also a small group of apples that fruit on spurs and tips, the so-called 'partial tip bearers'; these include popular varieties like *Bramley's Seedling*, *Worcester Pearmain* and the early *Discovery*. With these, it is a combination of trial and judgement: you can encourage the formation of spurs by treating the new laterals as if they were spur bearers – cutting back any new lateral that is over 20cm (8in) to three leaves above the cluster of small leaves around the base of the new shoot where it grows out of the branch. Leave any shorter laterals and tips unpruned for the fruit bud to develop.

It is important to find out how your trees produce their fruit, and to identify the requisite approach to summer pruning. The danger is that if tip bearers are pruned with the intention of creating fruiting spurs, then next year's fruiting buds will be pruned off and consequently there will be no fruit.

Fortunately, the majority of popular apple varieties are spur-bearers. For these, summer pruning for fruit consists of waiting until the terminal bud forms at the end of this season's new growth, then cutting back any of these new laterals that are over 20cm (8in) long, to three leaves above the cluster of small leaves around the base of the new shoot where it grows out of the branch. Any new laterals shorter than this should be left unpruned. Summer prune new growth from existing spurs back to just one leaf above the spur.

For tip bearers, once the basic framework of branches has become established, there will be little need for summer pruning; simply trim any long new laterals to 20cm (8in), leaving unpruned any that are shorter than this, as next year's fruit buds will be removed if the shorter laterals are pruned.

The shape and size of apple trees can be developed through winter pruning, when the tree is dormant. At this time of the year, without the leaves, the basic shape and structure of the tree can be seen, and any dead, diseased, crossing or badly placed branches can be removed. Winter pruning will also stimulate new growth when it starts in the spring.

Harvesting

Depending on the variety, growing conditions and the season, apples can be ripe and ready for picking from August through to the autumn, although some late varieties will hang on the tree until the New Year.

Early apples, like *Beauty of Bath*, *George Cave* and others, are probably best if picked and eaten straight off the tree as they ripen; they do not store well. They tend to have a soft texture, and once picked the skin gets softer; they bruise easily as they ripen quickly and the flavour starts to go.

Most apples come into season through September, with the main season peaking in October. Apple Day

Bramley's, at the back of the trug, harvested along with *John Downie* and *James Grieve* in early September.

is celebrated on 21 October each year, with apple-oriented events all over the country.

Late season dessert apples such as *Braeburn* or *Crispin*, and late cookers like *Newton Wonder* and *Edward VII*, will hang on the trees through October and once picked will store well and be perfect for use from the end of the year.

Apples are ready for picking when they come off the tree easily, when they are gently lifted in the hand. You should not need to pull the fruit off the tree, which can damage the branch and provide an entry point for disease. Another way of checking to see if an apple is ripe is to look at the pips: if they are still white, the apple will not be ripe – they turn brown as the fruit ripens.

Storage and Preserving

As mentioned, it is not worth trying to store early apples as they will start to deteriorate quickly in storage. With main season and later varieties it can be difficult to keep up with eating all of the fruit that the tree has produced, and storage or preservation will be the only way to save the crop for future use. Some of the later varieties of apple require a period of storage after picking so that they develop their full flavour.

There are a number of different ways in which apples can be stored, but they all have one thing in common: storage will only be successful if the fruit is in perfect condition, is not bruised or damaged by birds or insects, and shows no sign of rot. Once in store, apples must be inspected regularly to look for signs of rotting fruit, which must be removed immediately before it can affect other fruit nearby.

Different options for storage include:

Refrigeration: in a normal domestic refrigerator at 5°C, apples will keep for many months.

Traditional apple racks: a furniture-like structure, based on series of open slatted wooden shelves that slide in and out like drawers, on to which the apples are placed carefully in a single layer; traditional apple racks are themselves best kept in a cool, dark place like a cellar, garage or shed, where there is a good air circulation.

These *Newton Wonder* apples will be enjoyed for many months to come.

Wooden fruit boxes: as used by greengrocers; the apples are kept separate in a single layer, and the boxes should be stacked in a cool, dark place.

Polythene bags: use large, clear polythene freezer bags; pierce holes through them with a sharp pencil and into each bag place six or eight apples. Do not put more than that in any one bag or you risk losing the lot if one starts to rot. Then tie the top and store each bag in a cool, dark place; make sure that there is a good circulation of air, and check regularly for rotting fruit which must be removed immediately.

Apples can be preserved in a number of ways:

Freezer: raw apples should be peeled and quartered, dusted with sugar and dry-packed in polythene bags; cooked apples, stuffed and baked, in pies, crumbles or any favourite recipe, should be bagged or wrapped and then frozen.

Dried: fruit driers have been used in Europe for many years and are now becoming more widely available in Britain.

Wine: apple wine tends to be bland as the fruit lacks tannin, but if combined with a handful or two of elderberries to the gallon, the wine can be magnificent.

Chutney: apples make an excellent base for a wide range of different fruit chutneys.

Pests, Diseases and Problems

Apples can suffer from problems that affect all fruit, but there are a number of pests and diseases that are specific to apples. Listed below are common problems; please refer to the Pests, Diseases and Problems section within Chapter 4.

Aphids
Apple sawfly
Biennial bearing
Birds and beasts

Bitter pit
Brown rot
Canker
Codling moth
Drought
Frost
Honey fungus
Phytophthora
Powdery mildew
Scab
Winter moth and tortrix moth caterpillars

Recommended Varieties

There are thousands of varieties of apple: dessert or cooker; red, green or yellow; large, medium or small fruits; early, mid or late season. Most garden centres will stock a dozen or more of the most popular varieties, but the widest choice will be found in specialist nurseries, and it is worth tracking down some of the more interesting local varieties to bring something unusual and interesting to your garden.

Dessert Apples

Delbarestivale (also known as Delcorf and Delbard) (AGM): distinctive honeyed flavour makes this very special; also a good cropper. Season: September to October. Flowering group 3.

Delbarestivale.

James Grieve (AGM) – reliable cropper, very juicy and good flavour, early fruit cooks well, resistant to mildew. Season: September – October. Flowering group 3.

James Grieve.

Kidd's Orange Red (AGM): superb aromatic flavour, good-sized fruit, attractive skin colour and firm flesh. Season: November to January. Flowering group 3.

Kidd's Orange Red.

Pixie (AGM): good alternative to *Cox*, aromatic and crisp. Season: December to March. Flowering group 4.

Scrumptious (AGM): sweet, crisp and juicy; a good cropper with attractive red fruit; frost hardy and disease resistant. Season: August to September. Flowering group 3.

Worcester Pearmain (AGM): good cropper, nice looking fruit, good aromatic flavour, crisp to eat; some resistance to mildew. Season: September to October. Flowering group 3.

Worcester Pearmain.

Cookers

Bramley's Seedling (AGM): the most popular cooking apple and readily available in supermarkets, so why bother to grow it? It is an easy tree to grow and gives a good crop; it is a strong grower, a reliable cropper that will not disappoint, and nothing can beat the flavour of home-grown *Bramley's*. Season: early October to March. Flowering group 3, but needs two other pollinators.

Bramley's Seedling.

Howgate Wonder: a good garden variety, resistant to some disease; a good cropper, and a good keeper; not as acidic as *Bramley's*. Season: October to March. Flowering group 4.

Lane's Prince Albert: Season: December to March. Flowering group 3.

Newton Wonder.

Newton Wonder (AGM): sometimes considered as 'dual purpose' as it is not as acidic as *Bramley's Seedling*, but cooks to a glorious puree, and can be eaten once mature; tree is a very vigorous grower. Season: November to March. Flowering group 5.

Peasgood's Nonesuch (AGM): huge fruit which cooks to a light, lemon-scented puree; perfect for baking. Season: September to November. Flowering group 3.

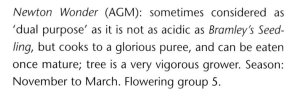

Peasgood's Nonesuch can grow to a huge size – here compared to a hen's egg.

Peasgood's Nonesuch is a glorious treat when baked.

Rev. W. Wilks: tasty fruit on a modest-sized, relatively compact tree, ideal for small gardens. Season: September to October. Flowering group 2.

Rev. W. Wilks makes a very large fruit.

Pollinators

Golden Hornet: small, attractive fruit that makes fine jelly, but its main strength is as a prodigious pollinator. Long flowering, across flowering groups 1, 2, 3, 4 and 5.

Golden Hornet.

John Downie: large fruit which are excellent for jelly, pickling and wine-making; can suffer from scab; in flower for a long time so will pollinate apples in flowering groups 1, 2, 3 and 4.

John Downie.

Apricots (*Prunus armeniaca*)

Apricot trees can produce a lot of fruit in the right conditions.

Despite their exotic image, apricots have been grown successfully in Britain for many years, and can often be found in the walled gardens of historic houses. Apricots have recently started to take off as a popular garden fruit with the introduction of new varieties that fruit more freely and are more suited to the British weather. In fact, apricot trees are a lot hardier than one imagines, and can be found growing in the high Himalayas as well as in Mediterranean climes. They tend to flower early in the year so their flowers may be affected by frost, and the cold conditions mean that there will be few pollinating insects, but these problems can be overcome by protecting the flowers when frost is forecast and using hand pollination to ensure a good fruit set.

As a fruit, the apricot is no more difficult to grow than, say, a plum, to which it is related, but the resulting fruit is much more likely to impress non fruit growers. They are also self-fertile, which means that you should get fruit from growing just the one tree.

Wall-trained apricots flowering in the March sun.

In addition to the sugars that make the apricot sweet, the fruit contains Vitamin C, beta-carotene and high levels of iron, as well as other trace nutrients. This means that eating your home-grown apricots is not only a glorious experience, but a healthy one too.

There tend to be fewer varieties available than for other tree fruit, but one or more of the recent introductions such as *Tomcot*, *Flavourcot* and *Delicot* should be available in most garden centres. Sometimes you may find the older, traditional varieties of apricot such as *Alfred* and *Moorpark*. Specialist nurseries will have a wider range from which to choose.

Once you have decided which variety to grow, there are several other factors that you need to take into account:

Shape and Size of Tree

While the shape of the tree is (mostly) up to you as the grower, and as the person who prunes and cultivates the tree to whichever shape or form that you want, the size will be influenced by the rootstock on which your chosen variety has been grown.

Most apricots on sale at garden centres will be grafted on to the semi-vigorous plum rootstock St Julian A, which is suitable for growing as a bush, pyramid or fan-shaped tree. Apricots will also be available on the slightly less vigorous rootstock Torinel, which will also be satisfactory for training in these different forms, but is most suitable for container growing. Some nurseries supply apricots grafted on to different rootstocks, so check the label before buying to make sure that the tree will grow into the form that you want. More information about rootstocks can be found in Chapter 1.

Because they flower early, and require a warm sunny position to ripen the fruit, apricots benefit from being fan-trained and grown against a south- or southwest-facing wall or fence. If an apricot is to be grown as a freestanding bush or pyramid, try to choose a relatively sheltered site that will receive plenty of sun. By growing an apricot in a container, the tree can be kept sheltered during the winter and then moved out into full sun once the fruit has set and needs to ripen.

The basic principles of fan training are covered in the information about growing forms and training in Chapter 1.

Pollination

In one sense, pollination is not a problem when growing apricots, as they are self-fertile. The only problem is that as they tend to flower early, they could be hit by frost, and there will not be many pollinating insects around at that time of the year. The flowers can be protected by covering the tree with horticultural fleece when frost is forecast during flowering time; just make sure that it does not touch the actual flowers and that it is removed once the temperature starts to rise so that if there are any insects around they can get to the flowers easily. To ensure a good fruit set, the flowers can be pollinated by hand using a small, soft, artist's paintbrush. Choose a warm sunny day when the flowers on the fruit tree are open fully and the pollen is 'ripe' – that is, when you can see dusty yellow pollen on the anthers of the flowers. Use the tip of the brush to transfer the pollen gently from the anthers to the stigma of the flower, which is usually located right in the centre of the flower, glistening and receptive to the pollen. To make sure that pollination is really effective, this operation may need to be done on a number of different days, as the flowers open and the pollen ripens.

Planting

The basic principles for planting fruit trees are very similar, and are covered in detail in the Apple planting section.

Special Notes for Apricot Trees

Apricot trees are sold either bare-rooted, containerized or container-grown. They grow better if the soil is deep and fertile, well drained, and slightly on the alkaline side of the pH scale. Apricots require full sun to ripen, and will benefit from the protection of a wall or fence, so fan-training is the best option.

Planting and support are the same as for other tree

Wall growing helps to protect apricots.

fruits, but if growing as a fan against a wall or fence, make sure that the rootball is planted about 22–25cm (9–10in) away, with the trunk leaning towards the wall or fence. This helps to make sure that the roots do not get trapped in the dry area at the base of the wall or fence.

Stake bush or pyramid trees securely to support the new tree as it establishes its root system and to reduce wind rock. The stake should be driven at an angle into the ground, avoiding the area of the roots, so that it meets the tree at a point half-way up the trunk at an angle of about 45°; tie the tree to the stake using a soft rubber tree-tie or garden twine. Make sure the tie is not too tight and check it regularly to make sure that it does not restrict the flow of sap as the tree grows;

also make sure that the tree and the stake do not rub together as this could damage the bark and provide an entry point for disease.

Fan-trained trees should be trained and tied to a system of support wires across the wall or a fence. The basic principles of fan training are covered in the information about growing forms and training in Chapter 1.

Once established, apricot trees growing in the ground will not need much feeding; just sprinkle a little sulphate of potash over the root area in February, or water in a high potash tomato fertilizer once the fruit has set. An autumn mulch that incorporates a little farmyard manure will give weak-growing trees a boost of nitrogen to help them put on some new growth. Container-grown apricots will need to have the top few centimetres of compost renewed each year, and because the nutrients will be washed out through regular watering, a slow-release general fertilizer could be incorporated in the top-dressing. Once the fruit has set, container-grown trees will benefit from a regular feed of high potash tomato fertilizer.

Do not stint on watering during dry periods. New plantings will need regular watering in dry periods to help establish their root structure; trees in fruit will start to drop the fruit if the tree becomes stressed through lack of water.

Cultivation

Apricot trees are usually planted in the ground, but on a dwarfing rootstock they will grow and fruit in

containers, such as large pots. Container-grown trees are available through the year and can be planted at more or less any time, but avoid planting once the fruit has set as there is a good chance that it will be lost as the plant goes into shock as a result of the replanting. The best time to buy and plant apricot trees is when they are dormant, after leaf fall in the autumn and before the new buds open in the early spring. Although planting can be done whenever the ground is accessible and not too wet, from autumn, when the ground is still warm, through to spring, try to avoid extremely cold periods as the trees will take longer to get established.

Apricots bear fruit on short shoots made the previous year, and on short spurs that have been developed on older branches. Some spurs may develop naturally, but summer pruning for fruit will increase the number of spurs and the size of the crop. Once the basic shape of the tree has been established, pruning for fruit will entail pinching out the growing tips of laterals as they reach about 8cm (3in) long, usually in May. Pinch any sub-lateral shoots back to just one leaf. The pinching-out process may need to be repeated if the apricot laterals produce regrowth. Any large pruning cuts should be treated with horticultural wound paint to prevent infection entering the wound. Like other prunus, apricot trees should not be pruned during the winter as this could allow silver leaf fungal spores to enter the wound and infect the tree.

Harvesting

To develop their full flavour, apricots need to ripen on the tree. Test the fruit for firmness as the colour changes from pale yellow to that special 'apricot' orange; some varieties develop a red speckle which indicates that they are really ripe. The fruit should be removed from the tree with a gentle twisting motion. Try to avoid bruising the fruit or damaging the tree by tearing off the fruit and creating wounds that will allow disease to enter.

Puget Gold apricots fruiting on short spurs.

Fan-training apricots against a wall helps fruit to set and ripen.

Storage and Preserving

Apricots are best eaten fresh off the tree, but they may be stored for a short time in a normal domestic refrigerator at 5°C, which will slow the ripening process.

Apricots freeze well, either baked or 'dry packed' raw, with the stones removed, in polythene bags; once thawed, they are best used for cooking rather than eating raw.

Pests, Diseases and Problems

Apricots can suffer from problems that affect all fruit, but there are a number of pests and diseases that are specific to apricots. Apricots also suffer from the same problems that affect plums and cherries. Listed below are common problems; please refer to the Pests, Diseases and Problems section within Chapter 4.

Aphids
Bacterial canker
Birds and beasts
Brown rot
Drought
Frost
Honey fungus
Phytophthora
Powdery mildew
Silver leaf
Wasps
Winter moth and tortrix moth caterpillars

Recommended Varieties

Apricots are self-fertile, so with just one tree you should be able to get a decent crop.

Alfred: an old favourite, reputedly less prone to die-back than some varieties; nice-sized juicy fruit with good flavour. Season: late July to early August.

Aprigold: usually sold as a dwarf tree aimed at patio container growing; despite its size, it is reported to produce a worthwhile crop of full-sized fruit. Season: late July.

Delicot: new variety similar to Flavourcot, but with a more subtle flavour. Season: August.

Flavorcot/Flavourcot: a new introduction, reputedly bred for the British climate, so it flowers later to avoid frosts (but still best to keep a watch on the weather forecast); large fruits ripen to orange-red. Season: August.

Apricot *Flavourcot.*

Moorpark (AGM): very early flowering and sometimes sold as *Early Moorpark*; an old variety, said to date from 1760; it has proved to be a reliable cropper, with large round fruit, excellent flavour. Season: late July to early August.

Tomcot: a new variety which grows large fruit that are full of flavour; particularly suitable for the British climate; masses of attractive flowers in the spring. Season: late July.

Apricot *Moorpark.*

Sweet Cherry (*Prunus avivum*), Acid Cherry (*Prunus cerasus*)

Techlovicka – a lovely sweet cherry.

Cherries have always been considered something of a luxury fruit. The old English varieties of sweet cherry had a notoriously short season, and were only in the shops for a short time, which meant that they were expensive and so were thought of as something rather special; the darker, acid cherries, epitomized by *Morello*, were the traditional basis of cherry brandy, itself a luxury drink. For the amateur fruit grower, sweet cherries have presented something of a challenge historically – they tended to grow into large trees needing lots of space and, as most varieties available were self-sterile, more than one tree had to be planted in order to get a crop. *Morello*, being self-fertile, was less problematic, but it still produced a relatively large tree and there was a limit to how the acid fruit could be used.

But things have changed. Imported cherries have brought down the price for a punnet of fruit, and the quality has improved as retailers demanded large juicy fruit that would appeal to customers and not show the effects of travelling round the world. As a consequence, most cherries sold in British shops tend to be large, dark red to black in colour, with deep red flesh. This in turn has spurred on commercial growers to develop different varieties that meet the needs of the trade and the customer, and the horticultural industry has sought to improve the range of varieties of cherry available for growing in Britain.

A lot of work has been done to develop rootstocks that reduce the overall size of trees, and the range

A tree-full of *Napoleon* cherries in the National Fruit Collection at Brogdale, Kent.

of varieties available has increased. This means that a cherry tree is now a reasonable proposition for the amateur fruit grower. The National Fruit Collection at Brogdale grows over 300 different varieties of cherry; not all of these will be available in garden centres, but specialist nurseries will have a wider range.

Once you have decided which varieties of cherry to grow, there are several other factors that you need to take into consideration.

Shape and Size of Tree

As with other tree fruit, the shape of the tree is (mostly) up to you as the grower, and as the person who prunes and cultivates the tree to whichever shape or form that you want, but the size will be influenced by the rootstock on which your chosen variety has been grown.

For many years the only cherry rootstock available was *Colt*. Described as 'semi-vigorous', it still produced trees up to 8m (27ft) but could be restricted to around 5m (16ft), which is still large for the average garden. The relatively recent introductions of the dwarfing Gisela 5 rootstock for trees up to 4m (13ft), and the very dwarfing Tabel rootstock for trees to 2.5–3m (8–10ft) has meant that sweet cherry trees are now available that are suitable for smaller gardens and easier picking. Cherries growing on the Tabel rootstock can even be restricted for container growing. Acid cherries tend to be less vigorous than sweet cherries, so will tend to produce slightly smaller trees.

When you buy a cherry tree from a nursery you will be able to specify which rootstock you want; from a garden centre or other type of retail outlet there may not always be a choice, or even an indication of which rootstock you are buying. If in doubt, ask and make sure that it is what you want or the tree could easily outgrow the space available. If information about the rootstock and tree size is not available, shop elsewhere. More information about rootstocks can be found in Chapter 1.

Cherries on dwarfing rootstocks can be restricted to a bush or half-standard tree, but many fruit growers choose to grow cherries as fans, as the size and shape of the tree can be managed more easily. The basic principles of fan training are covered in the information about growing forms and training in Chapter 1.

Pollination

Pollination is a real issue for growers of sweet cherries. Most are self-sterile, so a second variety will need to be grown nearby for pollination, but some varieties are incompatible and will not pollinate others. Some self-fertile varieties are available, but the solution for many fruit growers is to plant a *Morello* acid cherry, which is self-fertile and will produce a crop in its own right, but is also a suitable pollinator for sweet cherries in adjacent flowering groups. When buying cherry trees it is vital that the pollination requirements are checked and understood; the cherries that you buy must be compatible in terms of pollination and flowering groups, or there is a risk that no fruit will be produced. Again, *Morello* and other self-fertile cherries are the exceptions to this requirement for a second pollinator tree.

The pollination information and requirements and the flowering group should be shown clearly on the grower's label attached to the tree when you buy it. If they are not, ask for advice.

Planting

The basic principles for planting fruit trees are very similar, and are covered in detail in the Apple planting section.

Special Notes for Cherry Trees

Cherry trees are sold either bare-rooted, containerized or container-grown. They grow best if the soil is deep and fertile, well drained, and slightly on the acid side of the pH scale. Sweet cherries really need full sun to ripen and develop their characteristic sweetness, but acid cherries will tolerate some shade. It is said that acid cherries like *Morello* will even produce fruit if planted on a north-facing wall. This may well be the case, but the fruit will be better flavoured if it receives some sun to help it to ripen and develop its full flavour.

Do not stint on watering during dry periods. New plantings will need regular watering in dry periods to help establish their root structure; trees in fruit will start to drop the fruit if the tree becomes stressed through lack of water.

Cultivation

Cherry trees are usually planted in the ground, but on a dwarfing rootstock they will grow and fruit in containers, such as large pots. Container-grown trees are available through the year and can be planted at more or less any time, but avoid planting once the fruit has set as there is a good chance that it will be lost as the plant goes into shock as a result of the replanting. The best time to buy and plant cherry trees is when they are dormant, after leaf fall in the autumn and before the new buds open in the early spring. Planting can be done whenever the ground is accessible and not too wet, from autumn, when the ground is still warm, through to spring.

Sweet cherries produce fruit on buds at the base of young laterals from the previous summer. Summer pruning for fruit should aim to restrict too much vegetative growth and so encourage the development of fruit buds at the base of short laterals. The tips of vigorous new laterals are pinched out when they have made five or six leaves; this arrests vigorous vegetative growth and stimulates the formation of fruiting buds. These laterals are then shortened by pruning back to three buds from the main branches in the autumn.

Acid cherries bear fruit on the previous year's growth, similar to blackcurrants. Left unpruned, the fruits will be further and further away on the outside of the tree as the branches grow. To avoid this, acid cherry trees should have a proportion of their three- and four-year-old branches cut back each summer to encourage new fruiting branches to grow. Any large pruning cuts should be treated with horticultural wound paint to prevent infection entering the wound. Like other *prunus*, cherry trees should not be pruned during the winter as this could allow silver leaf fungal spores to enter the wound and infect the tree.

Fan training is an easier way to manage cherry

Late Amber cherries developing on short fruiting buds.

Cherries fan-trained against wires.

trees. The basic principles of fan training are covered in the information about growing forms and training in Chapter 1.

Fan-trained sweet cherries: once the basic fan shape has been achieved, summer prune laterals to six or eight leaves in early summer; cut these laterals back to four leaves before the end of August. Fruit should be carried at the base of these short laterals; any new shoots that are growing back towards the fence or wall must be rubbed out and removed in early spring. Like other prunus, sweet cherry trees should not be pruned during the winter as this could allow silver leaf fungal spores to enter the wound and infect the tree.

Fan-trained acid cherries: once the basic framework has been established, the technique used when pruning

for fruit is known as replacement pruning. The aim is to produce new fruiting laterals each year, for fruiting the following season, while removing the laterals from last year which have produced fruit this year. Starting with the basic fan-shaped framework, in April rub out any buds that are growing towards the wall or fence or directly out from the face of the fan; select strong new laterals on the top or underside of the main branches of the fan, spaced every 15cm (6in) or so apart – these will be the main fruiting laterals next year. Tie these to the support wires as they grow, and pinch out the tip once they reach about 45cm (18in) long; other laterals which are growing between those selected are surplus, and should be stopped at four leaves or removed altogether to improve air flow. It is the new laterals that have been selected and tied in that will produce fruit next year. In following years a new shoot will grow out from the base of these selected laterals, which will be tied in and fruit the following year; the original laterals are removed after the fruit has been picked, pruning back to just above the new shoot. This pattern is repeated each year, and is the same technique as used for wall-trained peaches.

Like other *prunus*, acid cherry trees should not be pruned during the winter as this could allow silver leaf fungal spores to enter the wound and infect the tree.

Harvesting

Cherry crops are precious, and need protecting from birds so netting is essential. Try to leave the fruit on the tree to ripen; keep a close watch on the fruit as it starts to change colour, and pick as required, cutting the stalk of each cherry with scissors or secateurs – do not tear the fruit from the branches as this could leave wounds that will allow fungal disease or bacterial canker to enter the wound.

Storage and Preserving

Storing cherries can be difficult as they tend to ripen quickly once picked. Cherries may be stored for a short time in a normal domestic refrigerator at 5°C, which will slow the ripening process.

Cherries freeze well, either cooked, or 'dry-packed' raw, with the stones removed, in polythene bags; once thawed, they are best used for cooking rather than eating raw.

Pests, Diseases and Problems

Cherries can suffer from problems that affect all fruit, but there are a number of pests and diseases that are specific to cherries, both sweet or acid. (Cherries are also affected by the same problems that can affect plums and apricots.) Listed below are common problems; please refer to the Pests, Diseases and Problems section within Chapter 4.

Maraschino **cherries ready for harvesting.**

Aphids
Bacterial canker
Birds and beasts
Brown rot
Drought
Frost
Honey fungus
Phytophthora
Powdery mildew
Silver leaf
Wasps
Winter moth and tortrix moth caterpillars

Recommended Varieties

There are hundreds of varieties of cherry and garden centres tend to stock the most popular varieties, but the widest choice will be found in specialist nurseries, and it is worth tracking down some of the more interesting local varieties to bring something unusual and interesting to your garden.

Sweet Cherries

Lapins, also known as *Cherokee:* large, dark red fruit; self-fertile. Season: late July to early August. Flowering group 4.

Lapins cherry.

Hertford (AGM): excellent flavour, large black fruit with flesh that is pinky-red, turning darker as it ripens; crops well, but is not self-fertile, so requires a pollinator; some resistance to bacterial canker. Season: mid- to late July. Flowering group 3.

Merton Bigareu: large and deep red, the classic cherry; crops well, but is not self-fertile, so requires a pollinator such as *Roundel Heart* or *Stella*. Season: July. Flowering group 3.

Roundel Heart: large and glossy red cherry, an old traditional variety that needs a pollinator such as *Stella* or *Sunburst*. Season: early July. Flowering group 3.

Stella (AGM): large, richly flavoured cherry, dark red to black; self-fertile and produces large crops regularly; looks so good that the fruit is a regular prize winner at fruit shows, but the fruit will split if inundated in wet weather. Season: late July. Flowering group 4.

Sunburst: large black cherry with rich, sweet, dark juice; self fertile. Season: mid- to late July. Flowering group 4.

Acid Cherries

Morello (AGM): the most widely available acid cherry, quite rightly so; excellent flavour for cooking, self-fertile, a good cropper and a good pollinator for sweet cherries. Season: late July to August. Flowering group 5.

Morello cherry.

Peach (*Prunus persica*) and Nectarine (*Prunus persica* var. *nectarina*)

Peregrine **peaches growing as a fan.**

Perhaps not grown as widely as apples, pears or plums, the peach, and its smooth-skinned variant the nectarine, will grow perfectly well in British gardens – and if you really want to impress friends and family, there is nothing like presenting home-grown peaches picked straight off the tree. Like the apricot, the peach tree is much hardier than one would imagine from the delicately flavoured fruit that it produces, and grown on a modern rootstock a peach tree is a nice addition to any fruit garden. Peaches tend to flower early in the year so their flowers may be affected by frost, and the cold conditions mean that there will be few pollinating insects, but these problems can be overcome by protecting the flowers when frost is forecast and hand pollinating to ensure a good fruit set. When grown outside, peaches will fruit and ripen better if grown against a wall or fence to give some protection from the weather and to provide a degree or two of extra warmth to aid fruit set and ripening.

On the scale of difficulty, peaches, like apricots, are not much more difficult to grow than, say, plums, to which they are related, but the resulting fruit is much more likely to impress non fruit growers. They are also self-fertile, which means that you only need to plant one tree to get fruit.

Although there are many varieties of peach and nectarine, there is only likely to be a limited range available in most garden centres, but specialist nurseries will be able to offer more choice.

Once you have decided which variety to grow, there are several other factors that you need to take into consideration.

Shape and Size of Tree

Because they flower early, and require a warm sunny position to ripen the fruit, peaches and nectarines benefit from being fan-trained and grown against a south- or southwest-facing wall or fence. Peaches will grow successfully in the open as a bush tree, but nectarines should be kept to the fan shape unless you have a particularly warm and sunny, yet sheltered position. Most peaches and nectarines on sale at garden centres will be grafted on to the semi-vigorous plum rootstock St Julian A, which is perfectly suitable for growing as a fan-shaped tree, growing up to 1.8m (6ft) high and 3.5m (12ft) across. Increasingly, peaches and nectarines are available in a fan shape, ready to plant, having had a couple of years' pruning and training at the nursery. Some varieties are available on an extremely dwarfing rootstock, designed to be confined to containers, and sold as 'patio peaches'; these have a novelty value but will not produce the size and volume of fruit that one gets from a peach tree planted in the ground.

Another reason for growing peaches and nectarines as a fan is associated with the need to protect the trees from the fungal disease 'peach leaf curl'. This disease

will cause the emerging leaves to blister, distort and eventually drop off; in addition to looking unsightly and weakening the tree, it also reduces the cropping potential. Protection takes the form of a covering that will prevent rain reaching the branches, buds and leaves on the tree from December until June, while allowing rain water to reach the roots. This can be achieved more easily when the tree is growing against a wall or fence as the whole of the back of the tree will be protected, and a polythene cover over the front of the fan will complete the protection.

Pollination

In one sense, pollination is not a problem when growing peaches or nectarines, as they are self-fertile. The only problem is that they tend to flower early so may be hit by frost, and there will not be many pollinating insects around at that time of the year. The flowers can be protected by covering the tree with horticultural fleece when frost is forecast during flowering time, but make sure that it does not touch the actual flowers and that it is removed once the temperature starts to rise so that if there are any insects around they can get to the flowers easily. To ensure a good fruit set, the flowers can be pollinated by hand using a small, soft, artist's paintbrush. Choose a warm sunny day when the flowers on the fruit tree are open fully and the pollen is 'ripe' – that is, when you can see dusty yellow pollen on the anthers of the flowers. Use the tip of the brush to transfer the pollen gently from the anthers to the stigma of the flower, which is usually located right in the centre of the flower, glistening and receptive to the pollen. To make sure that pollination is really effective, this operation may need to be done on a number of different days, as the flowers open and the pollen ripens.

TOP: **Peach blossom ready for pollination.**

MIDDLE: **Use a soft artist's paintbrush to transfer ripe pollen.**

BOTTOM: **Apply the ripe pollen to the stigma of another flower.**

If the peach tree is being protected from peach leaf curl by a large polythene sheet, this will tend to bring forward the opening of the flowers, but it will also prevent insects from reaching the flowers so either raise the polythene cover on dry sunny days when the flowers are open and insects are about, or be even more vigilant about hand pollination to ensure a fruit set.

Planting

The basic principles for planting fruit trees are very similar, and are covered in detail in the Apple planting section.

Special Notes for Peach and Nectarine Trees

Peach and nectarine trees are sold either bare-rooted, containerized or container-grown. They grow better if the soil is deep and fertile, well drained, and slightly on the acid side of the pH scale. They require full sun to ripen, and will benefit from the protection of a wall or fence, so fan training is the best option. Often peaches and nectarines are sold already in a basic fan shape; this initial pruning and training will have been carried out over the preceding couple of years by the grower, and is likely to be reflected in the relatively high price that tends to be charged for ready-trained peaches and nectarines.

Fan-trained peach against a wall.

Planting and support is the same as for other tree fruits. When growing as a fan against a wall or fence, make sure that the rootball is planted about 22–25cm (9–10in) away, with the trunk leaning towards the wall or fence. This helps to make sure that the roots do not get trapped in the dry area at the base of the wall or fence. Stone fruit need plenty of water at the roots once the fruit has set to make sure that it swells.

The fan should be trained to a system of support wires across the wall or fence. Tie the branches to the wires using soft rubber tree-ties or garden twine; the ties should not be too tight and should be checked regularly to make sure that they do not restrict the flow of sap as the tree grows.

The basic principles of fan training are covered in the information about growing forms and training in Chapter 1.

Once established, peach and nectarine trees growing in the ground will not need much feeding; sprinkle a little sulphate of potash over the root area in February, or water in a high potash tomato fertilizer once the fruit has set. An autumn mulch that incorporates a little farmyard manure will give weak-growing trees a boost of nitrogen to help them put on some new growth. Container-grown trees will need to have the top few centimetres of compost renewed each year, and because the nutrients will be washed out through regular watering, a slow-release general fertilizer could be incorporated in the top-dressing. Once the fruit has set, container-grown trees will benefit from a regular feed of high potash tomato fertilizer.

Do not stint on watering during dry periods. New plantings will need regular watering in dry periods to help establish their root structure; trees in fruit need water to develop the stone and flesh, and will start to drop the fruit if they become stressed through lack of water.

Cultivation

Peach and nectarine trees are usually planted in the ground, but on a dwarfing rootstock they will grow and fruit in containers, such as large pots. Container-grown trees are available through the year and can be planted at more or less any time, but avoid planting once the fruit has set as there is a good chance that it will be lost as the plant goes into shock as a result of the replanting. The best time to buy and plant peach and nectarine trees is when they are dormant, after leaf fall in the autumn and before the new buds open in the early spring. Although planting can be done whenever the ground is accessible and not too wet, from autumn, when the ground is still warm, through to spring, try to avoid extremely cold periods as the trees will take longer to get established.

Pruning

Peaches and nectarines fruit on new laterals that have been produced during the previous year, so once the basic framework has been established, the technique used when pruning for fruit is known as replacement pruning. The aim is to produce new fruiting laterals each year, for fruiting the following season, while removing the laterals from last year that have produced fruit this year. If this form of pruning is not done, the peach will grow more and more straggly, with the fruit on the ends of the branches as the new growth gets further and further away from the main part of the tree. The best way to grow peaches is as a fan against a wall or fence; once the basic shape and structure has been established, the aim of pruning is to stimulate new replacement growth each year for next year's fruit, and at the same time to remove last year's growth once it has fruited and the fruit has been picked. Starting with the basic fan-shaped framework, in April rub out any buds that are growing towards the wall or fence or directly out from the face of the fan; select strong new laterals on the top or underside of the main branches of the fan, spaced every 15cm (6in) or so apart – these will be the main fruiting laterals next year. Tie these to the support wires as they grow, and pinch out the tip once they reach about 45cm (18in) long; other laterals which are growing between those selected are surplus, and should be stopped at four leaves or removed altogether to improve air flow. It is the new laterals that have been selected and tied in that will produce fruit next year.

In following years a new shoot will grow out from the base of these selected laterals, which will be tied in and fruit the following year; the original laterals are removed after the fruit has been picked, pruning back to just above the new shoot. This pattern is repeated each year, and is the same technique used for wall-trained peaches.

Like other *prunus*, peach and nectarine trees should not be pruned during the winter as this could allow silver leaf fungal spores to enter the wound and infect the tree.

If the tree is being protected from peach leaf curl by a polythene cover, this will need to be removed during pruning and cultivation, and then replaced. This may sound arduous, but the protection is essential and the polythene cover will raise the temperature around the plant and help the fruit to develop and mature. By June the cover can be removed completely and stored for the next winter; removal of the cover will allow sun and air to reach the peaches directly. At this point it is worth netting the tree to protect the fruit from birds.

High levels of garden hygiene are required when growing peaches, as they are extremely susceptible to brown rot; all fallen fruit should be removed as soon as it is seen, to reduce the chances of reinfection of the fruit remaining on the tree.

Fruit Thinning

Thinning is an important part of cultivation for peaches and nectarines. The combination of insect and hand pollination means that they are likely to have set a heavy crop of fruit. If this is left without thinning, the crop may be numerically large but the individual fruit size will be small. Thinning starts when the fruit

Thin overcrowded fruits to make space for ripening.

is about the size of a marble; start by removing all fruit that is facing the wall or fence, as this will never ripen; where there are 'twins' – pairs of fruit that are touching – remove the one that is towards the back, leaving the one at the front; keep a close watch on the remaining fruit and remove any that show signs of rotting or that are distorted or have been pecked or damaged. Thinning need not be completed all at one time, but is best spread over a period of time so that you can see how the fruit is developing. The aim of thinning is to end up with a worthwhile crop of fruit that will ripen. During May thin the remaining fruit down to singles, about 10cm (4in) apart; at the end of June do a final thinning that reduces the crop to about 15–20cm (6–8in) apart. This may sound drastic, but the fruit which remains should be large and juicy, and of much better size and quality than had the fruit been left unthinned. Take great care when removing fruit during thinning – twist them away from the branch; do not pull them off as this can leave a wound in the bark, which could become an entry point for disease. It may be easier to snip the thinnings off the branch using small-bladed secateurs or scissors.

Harvesting

To develop their full flavour, peaches need to ripen on the tree. Test the fruit for firmness as the colour changes from pale green through yellow to red; some varieties develop a deep red flush which indicates that they are really ripe. The fruit should be removed from the tree with a gentle twisting motion. Try to avoid bruising the fruit or damaging the tree by tearing off the fruit and creating wounds that will allow disease to enter.

Storage and Preserving

Peaches and nectarines are best eaten fresh off the tree, but they may be stored for a short time in a normal domestic refrigerator at 5°C, which will slow the ripening process.

They are difficult to freeze raw, but if baked in a crumble they freeze well and can provide a wonderful taste of summer in the depths of winter.

Pests, Diseases and Problems

Peaches and nectarines are particularly vulnerable to peach leaf curl; additional cultivation suggestions to help prevent this problem are mentioned earlier in the Shape and Size of Tree section.

Peaches and nectarines can also suffer from problems that affect all fruit, but there are a number of pests and diseases that are specific to peaches and nectarines, which also suffer from the same problems that can affect apricots, plums and cherries. Listed below are common problems; please refer to the Pests, Diseases and Problems section within Chapter 4.

Aphids
Bacterial canker
Birds and beasts
Brown rot
Drought
Frost
Honey fungus
Peach leaf curl
Phytophthora
Powdery mildew
Silver leaf
Wasps
Winter moth and tortrix moth caterpillars

Recommended Varieties
Peach

Avalon Pride: a new variety that claims to have good resistance to peach leaf curl; crops well. Season: August.

Duke of York (AGM): early, white-fleshed peach, good size and flavour. Season: mid- to late July.

Peregrine (AGM): beautiful white-fleshed peach, with good flavour; crops well, so needs severe thinning to produce fruit of any size; raised in 1906 by Thomas Rivers of Sawbridgeworth, Hertfordshire, so well suited to the climate of southern England. Season: early to mid-August.

Redwing: dark red fruit, heavy cropper with good

Peregrine **peach.**

flavour; late flowering to help miss frost damage; claims some resistance to peach leaf curl. Season: August.

Rochester (AGM): yellow-fleshed fruit with reasonable flavour; flowers a bit later, which can help in frosty conditions, but still needs a warm sunny position to flourish. Season: early to mid-August.

Nectarine

Early Rivers (AGM): another splendid fruit from Thomas Rivers, this nectarine crops well and has a good flavour. Season: mid-July.

Lord Napier (AGM): dark red skin and white flesh make this an attractive fruit; juicy and tasty; raised by Thomas Rivers in 1869, so it has stood the test of time. Season: early August.

Pears (*Pyrus*)

Pears have probably been cultivated for as long as apples, and they remain a favourite for many fruit growers. A ripe pear is a real treat – juicy, with a buttery texture and an aromatic scent and flavour; eating a ripe home-grown pear is quite a different experience from the hard, crunchy supermarket pear. These pears are often picked when they are under-ripe and they never ripen and mature properly. One problem with pears is judging when they are ripe enough to eat; this is not so difficult when they are growing in the garden, where they can be checked every day, but more of a problem for shops that must have them picked, delivered and waiting for customers who will eat them at some point in the future.

To flourish and ripen well, pears require slightly higher temperatures than apples, and in cold areas the quantity and quality of the crop will be improved by growing the pear tree against a wall or fence. This will offer some protection from frost for the early flowers and reduce the potential for damage to new growth from cold winds in the early spring. Grown in this way the flowers will benefit from the added warmth reflected from the wall or fence, helping the pollen ripen and creating a better environment for pollinating insects. Once the fruit has set, the wall or fence will act as a storage heater and help the fruit to ripen fully.

Like apples, there are many varieties of pear to choose from, with over 550 varieties in the National Fruit Collection at Brogdale in Kent. Most garden

A tree full of pears is a lovely thing to grow in the garden.

Pears trained against a wall.

centres will stock a small number of the most popular varieties but a wider selection will be available from fruit nurseries. By choosing carefully, you could have ripe pears in the garden from August to December or even January. There are varieties that can be eaten as hand fruit, and others that appear to be rock hard until they are gently cooked to reveal their rich flavour. Whenever you have the chance, sample as many different pears as possible – this is the only way to make a fair comparison and will help you to choose which ones to grow in the garden.

There may already be a pear tree in your garden, or you may have a favourite that you would like to grow. Whatever the situation, take a moment to think through how to get the best crop and the best quality for your needs and your garden.

Once you have decided which varieties of pear you would like to grow, there are several other factors that you need to take into consideration.

Shape and Size of Tree

As with apples, although the shape of the tree is (mostly) up to you as the grower, and as the person who prunes and cultivates the tree to whichever shape or form that you want, the size will be influenced by the rootstock on which your chosen variety has been grown.

There are fewer choices of rootstock available for pears: essentially just Quince C, which will grow trees to about 3m (10ft), Quince A, for trees to about 3.6m (12ft), and BA29 for trees to about 4.5m (15ft), all depending on soil and growing conditions. Some growers are trialling and introducing new rootstocks that will increase the range of sizes for pear trees. As well as controlling the eventual height and vigour of the tree, the rootstock will also have some effect on how long you will have to wait before the tree starts to bear fruit, and on the size and quality of that fruit.

When you buy a pear tree from a nursery you will be able to specify which rootstock you want; from a garden centre or other type of retail outlet there may not always be a choice, or even an indication of which rootstock you are buying. If in doubt, ask and make sure that it is what you want – if not, shop elsewhere.

Pears on Quince A are probably a good general choice as they produce a strong tree with some vigour, which will only need controlling on the most fertile soils. It is better to have growing vigour to control in

a fruit tree, rather than trying to generate some vigour from a reluctant tree by using fertilizers.

More information about rootstocks can be found in Chapter 1.

Shape, Form and Training

Most pear trees sold through garden centres and nurseries will be one or two years old and will have already received some formative pruning and training to give them a general tree-like appearance. This is fine if you want to continue with this shape and form of tree, which will eventually grow into a larger version of what you buy, a tree or bush shape.

Ready-trained pear trees are sometimes available, usually espaliers. For single cordons and pyramids, or to do your own training, you will need a maiden tree

Single cordon pears showing extensive spur system.

Pear blossom in April waiting to be pollinated.

where the pruning and training has not yet started. These can be found in some garden centres, but are more commonly offered by nurseries.

More information about growing forms and training can be found in Chapter 1.

Pollination

All pears require a second variety for cross-fertilization to produce any fruit at all. So unless there are pear trees growing in neighbouring gardens, which can do the job, you will need to find space for two or three pear trees. For effective pollination choose pear trees from the same or adjacent flowering groups to make sure that they are all in flower at more or less the same time. If you are growing Catillac or another triploid pear, three trees will be required to complete the pollination cycle as the pollen from triploids will not be effective on other trees. A family tree, with different varieties growing on a single rootstock, is another way of making sure that effective pollination occurs.

The flowering group should be shown clearly on the grower's label attached to the tree when you buy it. If it is not, ask for advice.

Planting

The basic principles for planting fruit trees are very similar, and are covered in detail in the Apple planting section.

Do not stint on watering during dry periods. New plantings will need regular watering in dry periods to help establish their root structure; trees in fruit will start to drop the fruit if the tree becomes stressed through lack of water.

Cultivation

Pear trees are usually planted in the ground, but on a dwarfing rootstock they will grow and fruit in containers, such as large pots. Container-grown trees are available through the year and can be planted at more or less any time, but avoid planting once the fruit has set as there is a good chance that it will be lost as the plant goes into shock as a result of the replanting. The best time to buy and plant pear trees is when they are dormant, after leaf fall in the autumn and before the new buds open in the early spring. At this stage the shape and form of the plant can be seen clearly and any formative pruning required to shape the plant can

Embryo pear fruitlets.

Fruiting buds on a spur.

be done easily. Planting can be done whenever the ground is accessible and not too wet, from autumn, when the ground is still warm, through to spring.

Pruning

For general pruning advice please refer to the pruning section in Apples.

While there are a few varieties of pear that are considered to be tip bearers, the majority will fruit well from spurs created through summer pruning. This consists of waiting until the terminal bud forms at the end of this season's new growth, then cutting back any of these new laterals that are over 20cm (8in) long, to five leaves above the cluster of small leaves around the base of the new shoot where it grows out of the branch. Any new laterals shorter than this should be left unpruned. Any new laterals that are growing vertically upwards should be summer pruned to three leaves. Summer prune new growth from existing spurs back to just one leaf above the spur.

The shape and size of pear trees can be developed through winter pruning, when the tree is dormant. At this time of the year, without the leaves, the basic shape and structure of the tree can be seen, and any dead, diseased, crossing or badly placed branches can be removed. Winter pruning will also stimulate new growth when it starts in the spring.

Harvesting

Depending on the variety, growing conditions and the season, some varieties of pear can be ripe and ready for picking from August while some late varieties will hang on the tree until the New Year, but the main season runs from September through to early October.

Knowing when to pick pears is more of an art than a science, because by the time a pear on a tree appears to be ripe, it has probably passed the peak of perfection and is on its way to being too ripe to store. By the time they have changed colour from greenish to yellowish, and there is some 'give' when squeezed at the stalk end, the core is likely to have turned brown and the flesh will tend to be mushy rather than buttery. Pears can 'go over' very quickly, and can seem to change from being too hard to too soft within hours, if not minutes. This is all the more reason for keeping a close watch on home-grown pears, but through good timing you will end up with a superb fruit in optimum condition for eating. In general it is not a good idea to let pears ripen fully on the tree as the resulting fruit is likely to be disappointing.

In general, pears are ready for picking if they come off the tree easily when they are gently lifted in the hand. You should not need to pull the fruit off the tree, which can damage the branch and provide an entry point for disease. Changes in skin colour can be misleading, unless you become very familiar with the changes that the pears go through as they develop. All the pears on a tree will not become ready for picking at the same time, so you will need to check them on a regular basis, harvesting those that come away easily. Be careful not to bruise the pears, as this will hasten decay under the skin.

Very late varieties, which tend to be the cooking pears, will hang on the tree through to December without showing any signs of softening. The best plan for these is to leave them on the tree until the first one drops naturally, and then pick those that remain.

Storage and Preserving

Storing pears can be difficult, because, as mentioned under Harvesting, they can change and become inedible quite rapidly. The firmer, mid- to late season pears such as *Conference*, *Doyenné du Comice* and others, can be stored in the right conditions. Only attempt to keep perfect fruit that is not bruised and where the skin is fully intact and not damaged.

Pears can be stored in a normal domestic refrigerator at 5°C, which will slow the ripening process. Pick them early and check regularly to identify those perfect for eating, and those that have 'gone over', which should be thrown away before they affect others in store.

Like apples, pears can be laid out on racks in a cold store and kept for a short time, but again, check them regularly.

Once picked, pears can ripen quickly.

Do not attempt to store pears in polythene bags, as the moist atmosphere that develops in the bag will quickly lead to a bag full of rotten fruit.

The hard varieties of cooking pears will freeze well once cooked.

Pests, Diseases and Problems

Pears can suffer from problems that affect all fruit, but there are a number of pests and diseases that are specific to pears. Listed below are common problems; please refer to the Pests, Diseases and Problems section within Chapter 4.

Aphids
Biennial bearing
Birds and beasts
Brown rot
Canker
Drought

Frost
Honey fungus
Pear leaf blister mite
Pear midge
Pear rust
Phytophthora
Powdery mildew
Scab
Winter moth and tortrix moth caterpillars

Recommended Varieties

There are hundreds of varieties of pear but most garden centres will only stock a small number of the most popular varieties, ones that are relatively easy to grow and likely to produce a worthwhile crop. The widest choice will be found in specialist nurseries, and it is worth tracking down some of the more interesting local varieties to bring something unusual and interesting to your garden.

Dessert Pears

Concorde (AGM): a cross of *Doyenné du Comice* and *Conference*, which means the best of both parents: great flavour and a reliable cropper. Season: October to November. Flowering group 3.

Concorde.

Conference (AGM): bred for the British climate, this is the classic pear and crops reliably. Season: October to November. Flowering group 3.

Conference.

Doyenné du Comice (AGM): more successful if grown against a wall or fence, this is a beautiful pear with aromatic flesh. Season: October to November. Flowering group 4.

Doyenné du Comice.

Hessle: produces lots of small but juicy and tasty fruit; a good choice for cold wet areas. Season: September to October. Flowering group 3.

Hessle.

Merton Pride: delicious fruit, smooth and creamy flesh; this is a triploid, so two other pears will need to be grown nearby to complete pollination. Season: September. Flowering group 3.

ABOVE: **Merton Pride.**

BELOW: **Williams' Bon Chrétien.**

Williams' Bon Chrétien (AGM): fruits well in most parts of the country; another classic pear for flavour and texture; good resistance to disease, but it can be susceptible to scab. Season: September. Flowering group 3.

Cooking Pears

If there is room to spare it is really worth growing a cooking pear: as hard as a cricket ball, they will not be edible off the tree, but if poached gently for one to two hours they will turn into the most tasty pink fruit you can imagine.

Catillac (AGM): an ancient pear, with large flowers and large fruit; special taste when cooked long and slow; triploid, so requires two other pears nearby to ensure pollination. Season: pick October to November, store until January–April. Flowering group 4.

ABOVE: **Catillac.**

BELOW: **Black Worcester.**

Black Worcester: an ancient British pear which has been grown since the Elizabethan era and may even date from Roman times; a reliable and heavy cropper. Season: pick October to November, store until January–April. Flowering group 3.

Plums, Gages and Damsons (*Prunus domestica*, etc.)

Of all the fruits that grow in Britain the plum must be the one that gave meaning to the word 'fruitful' – few people can look at the vision of a plum tree laden with luscious fruit and not be impressed by this demonstration of nature's fertility in action.

Plums have been an important part of the human diet for many years – plum stones have been found at ancient sites and baskets of plum stones found in the wreck of the Tudor warship *Mary Rose* suggest that plums were a valuable part of the diet for British sailors.

Plums grow well in our climate and there are many varieties to choose from, especially when one includes related prunus fruits such as gages, damsons, cherry plums or myrobalan, bullaces and the French mirabelles, all of which are sometimes classified as 'stone fruit' by virtue of the fact that each individual fruit contains a single 'stone'. Plums are also closely related to apricots. With over 350 varieties of plum in the National Fruit Collection at Brogdale in Kent, it can be difficult to make a choice of what to grow – different varieties of plum may be large or small in size, in shades of red, yellow, green, blue, purple and black; some are perfect for eating raw, others take on another dimension of colour and flavour when cooked. There seems to be a plum for every taste. *Victoria* is the most popular, and probably rightly so – the fruit is large and juicy, with a good texture and

An abundant crop of plums.

flavour; they can be eaten raw or cooked, and are one of the most versatile fruits to grow. There may be varieties that are traditional to your local area. The opening up of Eastern Europe has seen many new varieties with distinctive flavours becoming available to British shoppers, and it is only a matter of time before they become available to gardeners, to add to our already rich heritage of plum varieties.

Most garden centres stock a small number of the most popular varieties but a wider selection will be available from fruit nurseries. By choosing carefully, you could be picking plums in the garden from late July through August and September. The best way to choose is to sample as many as you can, then pick the ones that you want to grow, to suit your taste.

There may already be a plum tree in your garden, or you may have a favourite that you would like to grow. Whatever the situation, take a moment to think through how to get the best crop and the best quality for your needs and your garden. Once you have decided which varieties of plum you would like to grow, there are several other factors that you need to take into account.

Shape and Size of Tree

As with apples and pears, the shape of the tree is (mostly) up to you as the grower, and as the person who prunes and cultivates the tree to whichever shape or form that you want, but the size will be influenced by the rootstock on which your chosen variety has been grown.

There is only a small choice of rootstock available for plums. The semi-dwarfing Pixy rootstock is best suited for growing plums as dwarf pyramids, cordons, bushes or trees up to about 3m (10ft) high and should produce fruit by the third year; the semi-vigorous St Julian A rootstock will grow up to 4.5m (15ft) and is good for general garden use. With more vigour than Pixy, it will get established without too much trouble, but it takes a year or so longer to come into fruit.

When you buy a plum tree from a nursery you will be able to specify which rootstock you want; from a garden centre or other type of retail outlet there may not always be a choice, or even an indication of which rootstock you are buying. If in doubt, ask and make sure that it is what you want – if not, shop elsewhere.

Plums on St Julian A rootstock are probably a good

Part of a massive crop that can be produced by *Belle de Louvain*.

Plum blossom in April.

general choice as they produce a strong tree with some vigour, which will only need controlling on the most fertile soils. It is better to have growing vigour to control in a fruit tree, rather than trying to generate some vigour from a reluctant tree by using fertilizers.

More information about rootstocks can be found in Chapter 1.

Plums grow and fruit well as bushes, half-standards or standard trees; grown as a pyramid they are very productive. They are also very successful if trained as a fan across a wall or fence, but if space is limited plums can also be grown as single cordons that do not take up much space.

The basic principles of fan training are covered in

the information about growing forms and training in Chapter 1.

Pollination

Most plums are self-fertile to some degree, so a crop will be produced by a single tree. However, there are some that require a second tree as a pollinator, so check the description and label when you buy. The size and quality of the fruit, and the overall crop, will be improved if there is a second prunus tree – plum, gage or damson – in the area. If you are planting more than one plum tree, pollination will be improved if they are from the same or adjacent flowering groups to make sure that they are all in flower at more or less the same time.

The flowering group should be shown clearly on the grower's label attached to the tree when you buy it. If it is not, ask for advice.

Planting

The basic principles for planting fruit trees are very similar, and are covered in detail in the Apple planting section.

Do not stint on watering during dry periods. New plantings will need regular watering in dry periods to help establish their root structure; trees in fruit will start to drop the fruit if the tree becomes stressed through lack of water.

Cultivation

Plum trees are usually planted in the ground, but on a dwarfing rootstock they will grow and fruit in containers, such as large pots. Container-grown trees are available through the year and can be planted at more or less any time, but avoid planting once the fruit has set as there is a good chance that it will be lost as the plant goes into shock as a result of the replanting. The best time to buy and plant plum trees is when they are dormant, after leaf fall in the autumn and before the new buds open in the early spring. Planting can be done whenever the ground is accessible and not too wet, from autumn, when the ground is still warm, through to spring.

Pruning

Newly planted plum trees are unlikely to need much, if any, pruning as they become established, and even then it will be a matter of keeping them to the basic shape and size required by just cutting back the leading branches in the summer. Unlike apples and pears, plums should only be pruned when they are in growth, and not during the winter months as there is a possibility of infection from the spores of the silver leaf fungal disease. Start to prune plums in June, making sure that all pruning is completed by

mid-August, and certainly by the end of the month. During this summer period there are fewer fungal spores around, the sap rising in the trees will help prevent any spores from entering the pruning cuts, and these wounds will heal more quickly. Any large cuts should be protected by immediately covering them with horticultural wound paint. Garden hygiene is paramount, so sterilize pruning tools before moving from tree to tree. If a plum tree becomes damaged at other times of the year and pruning is necessary, paint the cut with horticultural wound paint. Like all plants, plums that are kept healthy and strong growing will tend to be more resistant to problems like silver leaf and other infections.

Plums fruit on shoots that are one or two years old, on the established framework of branches. New shoots form readily, but can be encouraged by trimming any new laterals in the summer to about 15cm (6in), or the length of a pair of secateurs, to a downward-pointing bud. At this time central leaders can be cut back to a strong bud at the desired height, or to about half the previous summer's new growth – each spring choose a bud on the opposite side to the one chosen last spring, as in this way the central leader can be kept relatively straight. Main branches can also be cut back by about half of the previous summer's growth, or to a convenient length, to a downward-pointing bud – this will encourage horizontal growth, which is more likely to bear fruit. Remove any new shoots that are growing straight up from the horizontal branches as soon as they are seen, or you will find that there is a strong new branch growing up from the original branch, taking the vigour which should be used for fruit production. As they become established and get into the habit of fruiting, there will be less need to prune plums, unless you want to restrict the size of the tree; again, this should only be done during the summer months. Like other prunus, plum trees should not be pruned during the winter as this could allow silver leaf fungal spores to enter the wound and infect the tree.

Pull off any suckers that emerge from the rootstock during the summer or they will quickly become established and crowd-out the tree. Try not to cut suckers with secateurs as they will respond as if pruned, grow-

Plum flower buds about to break on a horizontal branch.

ing stronger and thicker. Pulling the suckers away will encourage the wounded rootstock to callous over so that regrowth is less likely.

Harvesting

Plum crops are sometimes so abundant that there is a real danger that the weight of fruit will damage the branches. The risk is increased if there is rain, which will add to the weight on the branches, or strong winds, when the tree is laden with fruit. To reduce the risk of damage, and to help prevent biennial bearing, thin the plums rigorously. Start after the initial drop of small fruit during May; continue to thin as the fruit swells through June by taking off any that show signs of damage or premature ripening as this is a sure sign that the fruit is infested by the larvae of the plum moth; do not leave fallen fruit on the ground as this

will support the life-cycle of the plum moth and cause further infestation the next year; fallen fruit will also encourage brown rot, which can devastate a plum crop. Do not compost fallen or rotting fruits, for unless high temperatures can be achieved in the compost heap the problem of plum moth and brown rot spores will be carried over in the compost. Continue thinning through late June and July, removing any fruit that become damaged or pecked, any with brown rot and any that are sticky and leaking. For large plums, aim to leave about 5–10cm (2–4in) between fruits – it may seem drastic but this will prevent the plums banging together in the wind and getting bruised; smaller plums can be left slightly closer together. Reducing heavy crops of plums lessens the likelihood of branches being broken under the weight of fruit, and should help to reduce the chance of the tree going into biennial bearing. Remember that the over-

Well spaced plums after thinning.

all weight of fruit will be more or less the same, but the fruit that remains will be larger and of better quality than if left unthinned.

Even after thinning some branches may still be heavily laden; these should be supported to prevent damage. Maypoling is one method – insert a sturdy stake into the ground, then support the branches individually with strings that run from the branch itself to the top of the stake, each branch having its own string support, giving the overall appearance of a maypole. Alternatively, support individual branches with a 'Y'-shaped prop, running from under the branch to the ground.

Plums for cooking or freezing can be picked when they are still on the firm side, but for dessert eating straight off the tree leave them until there is some 'give' in the fruit that indicates ripeness. Picking need not be completed all at once, but can be staggered over a week or so, picking the best plums as they become ripe.

Try to remove all the plums by the end of the picking season. Any left hanging on the tree risk becoming mummified over the winter; these become dry and full of brown rot spores, which will infect the tree during the spring and increase brown rot problems for the next crop.

Storage and Preserving

Storing plums can be difficult as they tend to ripen quickly once picked. Plums can be stored for a short time in a normal domestic refrigerator at 5°C, which will slow the ripening process. Pick them early and check regularly to identify those perfect for eating, and those that have 'gone over', which should be thrown away before they affect others in store.

Plums freeze well, either cooked or 'dry packed' raw – halved, with the stones removed – in polythene bags.

Pests, Diseases and Problems

Plums can suffer from problems that affect all fruit, but there are a number of pests and diseases that are specific to plums, which also suffer from the same problems that can affect apricots, peaches and cherries. Listed below are common problems; please refer to the Pests, Diseases and Problems section within Chapter 4.

Aphids
Bacterial canker
Biennial bearing
Birds and beasts
Brown rot
Drought
Frost
Honey fungus
Phytophthora
Plum moth
Powdery mildew
Silver leaf
Wasps
Winter moth and tortrix moth caterpillars

Plums affected by brown rot on their way to becoming mummified; these should be removed.

Heavy crops of plums can damage branches unless they are supported.

Recommended Varieties

There are hundreds of varieties of plum and gage, and gardeners really are spoiled for choice. Most garden centres will stock the most popular varieties, but the widest choice will be found in specialist nurseries, and it is worth tracking down some of the more interesting local varieties to bring something unusual and interesting to your garden.

Plums

Belle de Louvain: produces huge red fruit, excellent for cooking and acceptable as dessert fruit. Season: August. Flowering group 5.

Belle de Louvain.

Czar (AGM): self-fertile, a reliable volume cropper, a blue plum, should produce enough fruit to use and plenty to give away; good flavour, perfect for jam and acceptable for eating raw; some resistance to brown rot. Season: mid-August. Flowering group 3.

Jefferson (AGM). not self-fertile, but a good-flavoured plum, sometimes compared with gage; yellow flushed with red in colour; some resistance to brown rot. Season: mid to late August. Flowering group 1.

Marjorie's Seedling (AGM): vigorous and upright growing habit; self-fertile; crops reliably each year; blue plum, good for jam; some resistance to bacterial canker. Season: late September to early October. Flowering group 5.

Victoria (AGM): possibly the best flavoured plum; firm flesh perfect for cooking but also has an excellent flavour if left to ripen fully for dessert eating off the tree; self-fertile, so a reliable heavy cropper; reputed to show resistance to silver leaf if grown on the rootstock Pixy. Season: mid- to late August. Flowering group 3.

Victoria.

Warwickshire Drooper: self-fertile, reliable cropper; good for eating as a dessert fruit as well as for cooking; some resistance to bacterial canker. Season: early to mid-September. Flowering group 2.

Gages

These are smaller and sweeter than most plums, with a distinctive flavour, sweet and honeyed; generally, gages produce smaller crops than plums, but in a good year, a so-called 'Greengage Summer', the rewards will be magnificent. *Old Greengage* is thought to be a descendent from the original gage trees that were brought to Britain from France in 1742 by Sir William Gage. This is a tasty and interesting fruit to grow, but can be a 'shy cropper'; other varieties are likely to produce heavier crops.

Cambridge Gage (AGM): possibly the most reliable gage; sweet, with the classic gage flavour; partially self-fertile. Season: mid-August. Flowering group 4.

Reine Claude: the French gage, several varieties available; classic gage flavour; larger fruit than the *Cambridge Gage* and *Old Greengage*. Season: August. Flowering group 2.

Reine Claude.

Damsons (*Prunus insititia*)

Small, and intensely flavoured, the damson is usually too acid to be eaten raw, but cooks to a beautiful, rich red compote. If there is room in your garden, the damson will bring another dimension to your fruit and cooking.

All damsons are self-fertile, and some are sold unnamed on their own roots, but the following will produce good-quality damsons more consistently:

Farleigh Damson (AGM): produces heavy crops regularly; excellent flavour; flowers early but blossom shows some resistance to frost. Season: late August. Flowering group 4.

Merryweather Damson: named after the nurseryman who is credited with bringing the *Bramley's Seedling* apple into general cultivation, this produces small but highly flavoured fruit. Season: late August to September. Flowering group 3.

Common damson.

APPENDIX: A CALENDAR OF CARE – MONTH-BY-MONTH GUIDE

January

- Apply potash to soft fruit bushes, according to manufacturer's instructions.
- Continue winter pruning of apples and pears when it is not frosty.
- Keep peaches and nectarines covered to keep the rain off the branches, buds and leaves as they emerge in the spring, to protect from peach leaf curl; keep covers on until late May.
- New fruit trees and bushes can be planted when the ground is not waterlogged or frozen.

February

- Lightly fork over and loosen soils around fruit trees and bushes to break up the hard surface that will have been created by the winter; this will allow rain to penetrate more easily, rather than just running off the surface. This will also help birds forage for the pupae of gooseberry sawfly and other pests that have overwintered in the ground beneath the fruit.
- Apply potash to soft fruit bushes, according to manufacturer's instructions.
- Give all fruit growing in containers a feed of a general purpose fertilizer.
- Complete winter pruning of gooseberries and redcurrants.
- Prune established primocane autumn-fruiting raspberries and primocane blackberries down to ground level; cut newly planted canes down to a bud at about 25–30cm (10–12in) above the ground.
- Inspect fruit trees and remove any damaged or dead branches.
- Check that garden canes and ties supporting fruit are in good condition; replace as necessary.
- Inspect apple, pear and other fruit trees for signs of canker – flaky, sunken wounds on the bark of branches; cut out any affected areas, back to healthy timber, and burn the affected wood. Leave the treatment of plum trees until late March, or when the tree starts to come into growth.
- Continue planting new fruit trees and bushes when the ground is not waterlogged or frozen.
- Remove perennial weeds and clear the ground around the base of fruit trees.
- Protect any early flowering fruit from frost.

March

- Continue to protect fruit flowers from frost.
- Hand-pollinate flowers of peaches and nectarines on a warm day when the pollen is ripe.
- Winter pruning of plums can begin once they show signs of growth.
- Remove and burn any dead or withered tips spotted on cherry trees.
- Grafting, as a means of propagating tree fruits, can be started this month, as soon as the rootstocks show signs of coming into growth.

- The planting of fruit trees is usually completed this month, but container-grown fruit can be planted later in the spring, although this may shock the plant and delay it coming into fruit.
- Untie the canes of blackberries and other cane fruit that have been bundled together over the winter to protect from frost; train the untied canes on wires; apply potash to these and other cane fruits.
- Apply a high nitrogen fertilizer or farmyard manure to blackcurrants.
- Keep on top of annual weeds, removing them from around the base of fruit trees and bushes before they grow out of control.
- Strawberry runners, if available, can be planted out from this month.

April

- Be prepared to protect flowers and embryo fruit from frost on clear, cold nights; monitor weather forecasts and watch local conditions.
- Inspect gooseberries and redcurrants daily for signs of the first brood of gooseberry sawfly larvae eating the leaves; remove any larvae and deal with accordingly.
- Remove any branches of gooseberry or redcurrant bushes that have not come into leaf as they will have suffered from die-back or the effects of currant clearwing moth; burn or destroy any affected branches, do not compost.
- Inspect blackcurrants for signs of big bud mite (blackcurrant gall mite); remove and destroy any affected buds.
- Inspect pear leaves for signs of pear blister mite (small blisters on the leaves, which later turn black); remove affected leaves and shoots and destroy, do not compost.
- Inspect apples for signs of powdery mildew; remove and burn affected shoots.
- Aphid attacks are likely as the weather gets warmer. Either ignore them, and leave them to natural predators like blue tits and the larvae of ladybirds and lacewing, or control with horticultural soft soap if

the aphids get out of control and the natural predators cannot cope.
- Grafting should be completed this month.
- Finish planting new raspberry canes this month.
- Mulch to retain moisture in soil and irrigate fruit if rainfall is low.

May

- Continue to protect flowers and embryo fruit from frost on clear, cold nights; monitor weather forecasts and watch local conditions.
- Prepare pheromone traps for codling moth, raspberry beetle and plum moth as the weather starts to warm, and hang the traps near the fruit.
- Net soft fruit as soon as it starts to colour; do not forget to replace the roof nets on fruit cages.
- Continue checking for gooseberry sawfly larvae.
- Start thinning gooseberries towards the end of the month; use thinnings for an early pie.
- If American gooseberry mildew is spotted, remove affected shoots as part of summer pruning and consider spraying bush and fruits with a solution of washing soda.
- Lift developing strawberries off the ground to keep them clean and out of the reach of slugs, using straw or strawberry mats.
- Collect small, underdeveloped apples, pears and plums as they fall from the tree; do not compost as they may contain grubs, but dispose of by burning or in a local authority waste collection.
- Check the trunk and branches of fruit trees for woolly aphid, which appears as a small, fluffy, sticky white blob, congregating where branches meet the trunk, or in a line, spiralling up the trunk. Remove by wiping off and crushing the insect, or by painting the sticky blobs with methylated spirit which dissolves the sticky protection and dehydrates the insect.
- Remove pears that show signs of infestation with pear midge larvae – they will appear deformed and round in shape; if cut open, the cavity of the small pears will be black and filled with white larvae; dispose of by crushing or burning, do not compost.

- Start to thin apples and pears by removing any tiny, undeveloped fruit from clusters.
- Protect the newly emerging canes of summer-fruiting raspberries and hybrid berries; keep them trained away from the old canes so that they do not get damaged.
- Continue to irrigate fruit if rainfall is low; this will help fruit trees resist powdery mildew developing on the young shoots.
- Feed developing fruit with a high potash liquid tomato fertilizer.
- Keep down annual weeds by careful hoeing, taking care not to damage surface roots or the bark on the trees.
- Covers used for protecting peach trees from peach leaf curl can be removed at the end of the month.

June

- Continue checking for gooseberry sawfly larvae.
- Brut redcurrants and white currants to allow the sun to ripen the fruit.
- Summer prune gooseberries, removing the tips of shoots affected by American gooseberry mildew.
- Continue to collect and dispose of fallen fruit as the natural 'June drop' gets under way.
- Thin apples, pears, plums and other tree fruits.
- Pick strawberries, and remove any mouldy fruit so that it does not affect healthy fruit. Decide whether to keep runners as they emerge for propagation, and remove those that are not required.
- Protect floricane summer-fruiting raspberries from birds with netting; start to pick early fruiting varieties when ripe.
- Disbud wall-trained peaches and nectarines, and tie in shoots for fruit next year; remove any shoots that are growing straight back towards the fence or wall.
- Continue to loosely bundle the new shoots of cane fruit, which will produce the fruit next year.
- Remove and burn any dead wood that can be seen in cherry trees.
- Continue to irrigate fruit if rainfall is low; this will help the fruit to develop.

July

- Pick and enjoy gooseberries, redcurrants and other soft fruit when it is ripe.
- Summer prune blackcurrants at the same time as picking the ripe fruit.
- Continue thinning apples, pears and plums.
- Strawberry runners that have been kept should be pegged down into the ground or into pots filled with compost.
- Summer prune apples and pears once the terminal bud has formed on this year's new laterals; precise timing will depend on location and season, and may be staggered over a number of weeks.
- Complete the removal of any dead wood in cherry trees by the middle of the month.
- Pick cherries when ripe.
- Net peaches and consider protecting individual fruits with a soft muslin or paper bag to prevent damage from birds or wasps; pick and enjoy when ripe.
- Prop up or maypole heavily laden branches of plums to prevent the weight of the fruit from damaging the tree.
- Check tree-ties to make sure that they are not restricting the flow of water up the trunk; loosen if necessary.
- As soon as all the strawberries have been picked, remove and dispose of the large old leaves; clear old straw and mats out of the strawberry beds; remove and burn any diseased or stunted plants that may be suffering from virus disease.
- Budding, as a way of propagating tree fruit, can be started towards the end of this month.

August

- Pick and use soft fruit as it ripens.
- Pick plums, early apples, apricots and peaches as they become ripe.
- Remove the old canes of summer-fruiting raspberries once all the fruit has been picked; start to tie in and support the new canes that have emerged and will be fruiting the next year.

- Primocane autumn-fruiting raspberries are likely to be ready from this month.
- Check that strawberry runners have rooted and move them to their permanent position.
- Continue to look after the new growth on cane fruits; start to tie them in once the old fruiting canes have been removed.
- Summer prune plums and damsons after fruit has been picked; remove any dead wood from the trees.
- Consider netting apples and pears to stop birds pecking the fruit and giving an entry point for brown rot.
- Pick up fallen fruit and remove from the area around fruit trees; this will help maintain garden hygiene and break the cycle of brown rot, which will quickly develop on fallen fruit and then reinfect new fruit as the spores get splashed back into the trees when it rains.

September

- Remove the roof nets from fruit cages once all fruit has been picked, to allow natural predators such as birds to remove pests; in addition, the roof net will not collect falling leaves or snow later in the year, which can cause damage. (It may be advisable to keep primocane autumn-fruiting raspberries netted until picking has finished.)
- Complete the removal of old canes from floricane summer-fruiting raspberries and blackberry canes that have fruited this year.
- Pick and enjoy apples and pears.
- Apply grease-bands to the trunks of all fruit trees by late September to trap the female winter moths and prevent them climbing the trees to lay their eggs during October.
- Any budding should be completed this month.
- Winter pruning of gooseberries, redcurrants and blackcurrants can be started once the leaves have fallen; it can be left until the New Year so that any winter damage can be pruned out at the same time.

- Gooseberries, redcurrants and blackcurrants can be propagated from hardwood cuttings: take pencil-thick 25cm (10in) lengths of this year's new growth, with all but the top buds removed, and insert into a 20cm (8in) deep slit in the soil.
- Keep clearing fallen fruit away from the trees.
- Start thinking about what fruit you would like next year; do the research and planning, and place orders with specialist nurseries.

October

- Pick and enjoy apples and pears; select perfect, sound apples for storage.
- Remove all large figs that have not ripened this year, leaving any that are about the size of a garden pea – these embryo figs will swell and ripen next year.
- Bundle together the new canes of blackberries and other hybrid berries after leaf fall, and tie them loosely to one of the support wires to protect the growing tips from the cold.
- Clear fallen leaves from around fruit trees and bushes to maintain garden hygiene, or leave to provide shelter overwinter for ladybirds and other beneficial insects; clear fallen fruit.
- Begin planting new fruit trees and bushes while the ground remains warm.

November

- Continue planting new fruit.
- Finish picking any late apples or pears.
- Cover peaches and nectarines to keep the rain off the branches, buds and leaves as they emerge next spring to protect from peach leaf curl; keep covers on until late May next year.
- Winter pruning of apples, pears and other tree fruits can be started once leaves have fallen, on dry, frost-free days.
- Apply a light dressing of farmyard manure, if used, around tree fruit. This is especially useful for blackcurrants.

- Make sure that the roof nets have been removed from fruit cages before it snows.

December

- Pick any very late apples that are still clinging to the bare branches.
- Continue winter pruning when conditions are right.
- With the trees free of leaves, remove any 'mummified' fruit that can be seen clinging to the branches.
- Check stakes, supports and ties to make sure that they will stand up to the winter.
- Check fruit in store and remove any that show signs of rot or decay.

Seasons

Gardening books and plant labels often refer to 'seasons' – early, mid- and late – but what does this mean?

With climate change and extreme weather conditions in evidence the 'traditional' seasons of winter (December to February), spring (March to May), summer (June to August) and autumn (September to November) may remain a useful general guide, but the weather conditions that can be expected each month seem to vary widely from year to year. Watch and listen for up-to-date weather forecasts on the radio, television and dedicated websites, especially at blossom time when frost warnings are extremely valuable. In some years the seasons are reported as being early, in other years they can be relatively late, but do not worry too much about this. Fruit trees, like other plants in the natural world, will be able to cope perfectly well, speeding up or slowing down their development in response to the prevailing weather conditions. In a late, cold spring, blossom and leaf development may also be late, and when spring comes early the blossom may also be out and over early; but in both cases the metabolism of the plant will compensate and make sure that its fruit will be ready at more or less the same time each year. It's

nature, and there is little that fruit growers can do about it. Keeping records of weather conditions for your garden is a good way of tracking what is likely to happen as certain weather patterns develop. In fact, the more aware you become of how the weather affects your own garden, the more able you will be to forecast extremes and take the necessary steps to protect your fruit. Just remember: a bright day, clear skies with no cloud cover, and no wind, at any time up to June, and there could be a radiation frost overnight.

In terms of fruit-growing seasons, other factors can also have a great impact on how your fruit develops. One such factor is your location within the country – north or south, east or west; another is the height of the land above sea level. Even such basic differences as being on the north or south side of a hill, in a sheltered valley or in a 'frost pocket', will affect the growth and development of the plant.

In the south of the UK the soft fruit season can start as early as mid-June, and be all over by the end of July. Travelling north, up the country, the season will get progressively later, meaning that the soft fruit season may not start until mid-July, but may extend to the end of August.

Some of the descriptions given by growers can be misleading: an 'early' gooseberry ripens in June, but an 'early' apple will not be ripe until August; likewise, a 'late' summer-fruiting raspberry will be ripe in August or September, but a 'late' apple will not be ready to pick until November or even December.

Given that it is impossible to be definite about the precise dates for the seasons for every type of fruit in every garden in every growing situation, all you can do is be guided by the seasonal descriptions given by growers, in the context of your own garden: 'early' will be the first to open or ripen, 'late' or 'very late' will be the last. With a little planning and careful selection you should be able to have a succession of fruit across the entire season, early, mid- and late, with one variety coming into fruit as another comes to its end. Keep your own notes of flowering, fruiting and picking dates, weight of crop, etc., as these will prove to be a most valuable way of monitoring the growth and development of your fruit from year to year.

GLOSSARY

AGM (Award of Garden Merit) – an award given by the Royal Horticultural Society (RHS) to plants that in trials have proved to grow and perform well in general garden conditions, and that have some resistance to pests and disease.

Backfilling – the act of replacing soil that has been removed from a planting hole around the roots of the tree or bush as it is being planted.

Bare-rooted – fruit trees and bushes will be supplied bare-rooted if they are dug straight from the propagation beds at a nursery, with very little soil clinging round the roots. They are likely to be wrapped in damp hessian to keep the roots alive, or in a bag or pot, containerized and covered loosely with damp compost. Bare-rooted plants tend to grow away better in the ground once replanted, as they have never had their roots restricted during pot growing, so can cope better with garden soil conditions.

Biennial cropping – when a fruit tree produces a crop only every other year. This is usually the result of the tree carrying a very heavy crop one year, exhausting its strength, and consequently producing a very small crop the following year. If fruit trees are left unthinned, they will attempt to produce as many fruits as possible, resulting in a very heavy crop of small fruit – this is likely to lead to biennial cropping. The answer is to thin the crop severely (see Thinning).

Brutting – the term used to describe the summer pruning of redcurrants; the action of snapping off about half the length of the new season's growth on the laterals across the blunt back of a pruning knife, or across the unopened blades of secateurs, as opposed to using the sharp blade to make a pruning cut. The action of snapping, rather than cutting, seems to prevent regrowth and nutrients that would otherwise go to leaf production go to helping the fruit to swell.

Bush fruit – general term used to describe different fruits that tend to be grown in bush form, such as blueberries, currants, gooseberries, etc.

Bush tree – a young (two- or three-year-old) tree that has been pruned to form a typical tree shape with three or four main branches.

Cane – term used for the long growing shoots and stems of ribes fruit, such as raspberries, blackberries and other hybrid berries. This is distinct from bamboo canes, which are used to support fruit and other plants.

Cane fruit – includes blackberries, raspberries and hybrid berries such as loganberry, tayberry, wineberry, sunberry, etc.

Container-grown – fruit trees and bushes that have been grown in pots since they were propagated, so may take some time to acclimatize to soil conditions when planted; roots may have grown round the inside of the container; soak well before planting, and tease out the roots carefully to help them get established in the ground, or there is a danger that the roots will continue to grow round and round in a tight bundle and will then be susceptible to lack of water.

Containerized – fruit trees and bushes that have been field grown, lifted and put into pots of compost for sale.

Cordon – a restricted form of growing fruit, ideal for packing lots of different varieties into a relatively small space. A single cordon does not have branches as such, but is kept as a single leader where the fruit will be borne on spurs or short laterals growing along the length of the cordon; this form of growing can be trained, depending on space, into double or even triple cordons, with two or three leaders, each bearing fruit; a cordon requires permanent support throughout its life, and regular summer pruning to maintain fruit production; cordons may be grown vertically, or down to an angle of 45° depending on space, the vigour of the particular fruit and rootstock, and the look that you want to achieve in your fruit garden. *Minarette* and *Ballerina* fruit trees are, in effect, ready-made, vertical single cordons.

Cultivar – botanically, a cultivar is a plant of the same species that has been developed as a result of crossbreeding or the positive selection of particular characteristics during cultivation; for example, *Fiesta* is a modern apple cultivar that was developed by crossing *Cox's Orange Pippin* with *Idared* in the 1970s; in general gardening, the term tends to be used interchangeably with variety.

Diploid – refers to trees having two matched pairs of chromosomes, creating an even number, and resulting in trees that are self-fertile to some degree but also produce pollen that will cross-pollinate other trees of the same type; most fruit trees are diploid.

Downward-pointing bud – a bud that is generally pointing down, towards the ground.

Drupelet – one of the many small yet individual fleshy parts, each containing a seed, that make up a whole aggregate fruit such as a raspberry or blackberry.

Espalier – a decorative yet highly productive form of training fruit trees against wires, walls or fences, where the fruit is borne on pairs of horizontal branches that are trained out from the central vertical leader; most commonly used for apples and pears.

Family tree – a single fruit tree on to which has been budded or grafted two, three or more different varieties; the varieties will have been chosen to make sure they pollinate one another for maximum fruit set; each variety will grow on its own branches and so a single tree can provide a number of different types of apple. The ultimate family tree stands in Sussex. It started as a *Bramley's Seedling*, and now has 250 different varieties of apple budded or grafted on to the main framework of the tree – possibly a world record.

Fan – a decorative form of training fruit, where the branches radiate out across wires, walls or fences like the fingers on a hand, from a low-cut central point; fan training is suitable for redcurrants, gooseberries and cane fruit, as well as tree fruit such as apples, pears, cherries and plums.

Feathered maiden – a young, unpruned tree, principally a single leader, that has put on a number of longer laterals, probably into its second year.

Field grown – fruit trees and bushes that have been grown outdoors in the soil since they were propagated, which means that they will establish quickly when planted into a garden; often sold bare-rooted, but sometimes lifted and sold in pots as containerized trees.

Floricane – literally, the growth that a cane fruit produced in the previous year, now in its second year and ready to flower and fruit; in practice this term is used to describe the fruiting habit of most cane fruit such as blackberries, raspberries and hybrid berries, which produce fruit on canes that have grown during the previous year. Cultivation of floricane varieties is based on looking after and keeping the new canes as they grow each year, and removing the old canes after the fruit has been picked, making room for the new canes which will fruit next year.

Frost gate – a gap in the hedge or fence around a frost pocket, through which cold air can drain away.

Frost pocket – a low area of land into which cold air sinks and cannot escape; an area to be avoided when planting fruit unless a frost gate can be arranged.

Fruit cage – a netted enclosure that is designed to protect fruit growing inside the cage from birds; most will be a permanent structure over an area of garden, with stiff netting around the sides and having a door for access; the top will remain uncovered during the autumn and winter to prevent damage from the weight of leaves or snow, and into the early spring to allow natural predators such as blue tits to help remove pests such as aphids and caterpillars; as soon as the fruit starts to change colour and ripen, the top of the fruit cage is covered with a soft, flexible net, to prevent the fruit being eaten or damaged by birds; once the top net has been fixed in place, care must be taken to make sure that the door is kept closed and the side netting is fixed at ground level to stop birds squeezing under the net and getting trapped inside the cage; fruit cages are particularly useful for growing soft fruits that are attractive to birds, such as redcurrants, and tree fruits such as cherries, which will be stripped from the branches by birds unless they are protected. Although they can be as great an investment as a garden shed, a fruit cage gives the fruit grower the reassurance that their fruit is protected at all times.

Fruit set – the change from fertilized flowers to fruit; 'high' or 'low' fruit set is used to describe how well the flowers have been pollinated and how heavy the fruit crop is likely to be.

Half-standard – a young tree with a clear stem of about 1.2–1.5m (4–5ft) from planting level to a head of branches.

Horticultural wound paint – a proprietary 'paint' that is sold to apply to pruning cuts or areas where cankers have been removed; it is designed to protect the cut surface from infection; not necessary for all pruning tasks, but particularly useful for protecting exposed areas of branch after cutting out cankers and for protecting any wounds on plum trees during the winter months.

Laterals – new growth out from the sides of branches, bearing leaves and filling in the overall shape of the tree; in some fruits the laterals carry the fruit, either along their length or at the tips; in others, the laterals are summer pruned to form fruiting spurs where the buds develop into fruit.

Leaders – new shoots, up to one year old, growing from the ends of the main branches that form the structure of the fruit tree or bush; most plants will have a strong growing central leader from which the other leading branches radiate or grow; cordon-grown trees will consist of little more than a central leader with short laterals or spurs; some other forms of trained fruit trees, for example fans, will have the central leader pruned out so that the vigorous growth that the tree would otherwise be putting into its central leader is diverted into other buds and used to stimulate the formation of the ribs that form the fan.

Leg – the length of bare stem or trunk between the soil and where the branches start to radiate out from the central leader.

Maiden – young tree in its first year, at the end of its first season after being grafted or budded; usually a single leader that has never been pruned, with a few feathery laterals; a maiden tree can be grown and trained into whichever form is required.

Maiden whip – a young, unpruned tree in its first year after budding or grafting; principally a single leader that has few if any laterals.

Maypoling – a way of supporting heavily laden branches of fruit by inserting a sturdy cane or stake into the ground near the centre of the bush, then supporting branches individually with strings that run from the branch itself to the top of the cane, each branch having its own string support, giving the overall appearance of a maypole.

Mulch – a layer on the ground or around a tree that will help to retain moisture in the soil; natural mulches include compost, grass clippings, sterilized bark or shredded pine clippings; artificial mulches include black polythene sheet, weed-suppressing membranes, even a thick layer of newspaper. With all mulches, try to make sure that it does not come into direct contact with the trunk of the tree as this could create a site for the entry of fungal disease.

Mummified fruit – these are old, shrivelled fruits that remain clinging to the branches during the winter; having rotted and dried on the tree they will be full of fungal spores, which will infect the newly emerging growth in the spring; mummified fruit should be removed when seen, which is easiest during the winter when there are no leaves on the trees.

Oblique cordon – a cordon being grown at an angle to the ground, rather than upright; the angled nature of its growth helps to encourage the formation of fruit buds. The 'traditional' angle for oblique cordons is 45° to the ground but, depending on spacing and the vigour of the cordon, the angle could be anywhere between 45° and 60°. Lowering the angle will reduce the vigour; raising it more towards the vertical will increase the vigour of growth.

Outward-facing bud – a bud that is pointing in any direction away from the centre of a tree or bush.

pH – the chemical measurement of acidity. In the garden context it is a useful indication of how suitable the soil is for growing plants that may have particular requirements in terms of the acidity of the soil; pure water is regarded as being neutral, with a pH of 7; a pH less than 7 is said to be acidic, while higher than 7 is considered to be alkaline. The only way to be certain about the pH of the soil is to test it – either using a DIY kit, available at most garden centres, or by sending it to a soil-testing laboratory. The key thing about testing is to take samples from different places to get an overall picture of the garden, rather than test just one spot which may or may not be typical of the garden as a whole.

Pinching out – the practice of using the thumb and fingers to remove buds or soft growth from the tips of branches; an alternative to using a knife or secateurs when the plant tissue is soft, before it turns into hardwood.

Primocane – literally the current year's growth that a cane fruit puts on through the spring and early summer, resulting in new canes; in practice this term is used to refer to plants that bear fruit on canes produced in the current year, such as autumn-fruiting raspberries, and some new varieties of blackberry that are starting to become available to the amateur gardener. Cultivation is based on cutting down the old canes that fruited last year in the late winter, and encouraging new canes to grow through the spring and early summer to produce this year's fruit crop.

Puddling, puddling-in – pouring water into the planting hole and around the roots as a tree is being planted; the idea is to wash soil around the roots so that it makes contact with the roots and does not leave any air pockets, which would prevent the roots from taking up nutrients.

Replacement pruning – once the basic framework of a fan-trained fruit tree has been established, this is the technique for producing new fruiting laterals each year, for fruiting the following season, while removing the laterals from last year that have produced fruit this year; this technique is used for fan-trained acid cherries and peaches.

Ripe wood – used to describe new growth that has matured through the growing season, as a result of ageing and the action of sun and the weather; it will have changed from being greenish, soft and pliable to become harder and ready for the development of fruiting buds.

Rootball – the soil or compost that clings around the roots of a plant when it is lifted from the ground or removed from a container; the living roots of the plant that will be taking in nutrients.

Rootstock – most fruit trees are produced by budding or grafting a named variety on to a rootstock, the part of the tree that is planted into the ground; it is the rootstock that determines the size and vigour of the particular variety of fruit that is growing on the top of the tree. In addition to size and vigour, the rootstock will also have some bearing on how many years it takes before the tree starts to produce fruit, and to some extent the size of the fruit produced. Different rootstocks suit different growing conditions; some have particular soil or cultivation requirements to grow at their best, and some may have particular needs in the way they are supported or trained.

Russetting – seen as a roughened, dull, matt area on the skin around the top of fruit such as apples and pears; russetting may be a natural feature of the fruit, such as a russet apple, or it may be caused if the fruit has been damaged by frost.

Shy cropper – a fruit that does not always produce a worthwhile crop, but will produce a crop when conditions meet its particular requirements for flowering time, pollination, rainfall and sun to ripen; shy croppers tend to be grown for their distinctive qualities, such as a superb flavour, rather than for the volume they produce; a good example of a 'shy cropper' would be *Old Greengage.*

Soft fruit – a general term used to refer to summer fruits, usually berries, which tend to be soft or crush readily, such as blackberries, blueberries, currants, gooseberries, raspberries and strawberries.

Soft soap – sometimes called insecticidal or horticultural soft soap, and based on non-toxic biodegradable fatty acids, this is used as a spray for dealing with heavy infestations of aphids that cannot be controlled by natural predators.

Sport – a seedling or sucker that differs from its parent plant; they usually occur spontaneously.

Spurs – a lateral that has been pruned short, which bears a fruit bud or a rosette of leaves at its tip.

Spur bearer – a tree that produces its fruit on spurs, which should be summer pruned to encourage the formation of more spurs and consequently more flowers and fruit.

Spur pruning – the operation of creating a spur from a lateral, by pruning back the lateral to a bud at 7.5–10cm (3–4in) in its first year, or less, depending on the fruit being pruned, and then to a bud at 2.5cm (1in) in each subsequent year, building up a spur system.

Spur system – a build-up of a number of spurs on the same lateral, as a result of repeated summer pruning. Over time, a long or complex spur system may need to be reduced by pruning back to a point closer to the branch, to avoid damage and to maintain the development of fruit buds and the quality of fruit – this process is known as spur-shortening.

Standard – a young tree with a clear stem of about 1.8m (5ft) or more from planting level to its head of branches.

Stepover – a cordon that has been trained to the horizontal at a height where it is easy to pick the fruit and tend to the pruning.

Strig – the hanging clusters of flowers or fruit that form on currants; a strig may be just a few millimetres long on some blackcurrants, but may be up to 10cm (4in) on some redcurrant varieties.

Stooled bush – bushes where the new shoots come straight out of the ground, rather than radiating out from a central leg or trunk; this form of bush is produced by cutting old growth to ground level, and feeding well to encourage new growth from below ground level.

Stub – a short, bare length of branch left above a bud after pruning, which can occur if the pruning cut is not made close enough to a bud; it is not good pruning practice to leave stubs as the short length that is left is likely to die back, it will not produce any more buds and could become a host for fungal infections such as coral spot, which can affect the rest of the branch.

Sub-laterals – short new growths on the laterals, which sometimes occur after summer pruning.

Suckers – new growth which comes from the roots of the plant, sometimes at some distance from the original plant; if left to grow, suckers from fruit trees on rootstocks will have the characteristics of the rootstock rather than the fruit that is growing on the rootstock; if left to grow and set fruit, they may produce something unusual, but almost certainly it will be inferior. Where a rootstock is not involved, as with cane fruit, a runner will fruit like the parent plant, but over time there may be some deterioration in quality as virus disease takes hold. Unless a runner is required for propagation it should be removed. This is best done by digging down to the site where the runner is growing out from the root, and pulling it from the root – cutting a runner will have the same effect as pruning, and it is likely to grow back bigger and stronger than before. Dust any wounds made to the roots with yellow sulphur powder to reduce the risk of fungal infection when the soil is replaced.

Thinning – the removal of immature fruit to reduce the total number of fruits allowed to develop to maturity. This is done to reduce the stress on a tree that is over-laden with fruit, to reduce the chance of the tree going into biennial cropping, and to improve the overall size and quality of the fruits that remain after thinning. Thinning can be very stressful for a fruit grower, as it sometimes seems that more of the precious fruit is being removed than is left on the tree. However, research has shown that, although there may be fewer individual fruits left on a tree, the total weight of fruit produced will be the same as for a tree that has not been thinned. This means that the individual fruits will be larger and heavier; conversely, although there may be more individual fruits on a tree that has not been thinned, they will each be smaller. Fruits that are diseased or infested with maggots can be removed effectively during thinning – it has been noted, for example, that the first plums to show signs of ripening are often the ones that contain a plum moth maggot – these are the ones to thin out first.

Thinnings – the fruit that has been removed during the process of thinning.

Tip bearer – a fruit tree that bears its fruit on the tips of short laterals grown from the main branches in the previous season; tip bearers include some apples and pears and all quince.

Top-dressing – feeding the soil or compost from the top by adding a layer of new, fresh compost or fertilizer; in the case of container-grown fruit replacing the top few centimetres of old compost each year with new, fresh compost.

Top fruit (as Tree fruit) – a general term used to refer to fruits that grow on trees, such as apples, pears, plums, peaches, apricots, quinces, etc.

Tree fruit (as Top fruit) – a general term used to refer to fruits that grow on trees, such as apples, pears, plums, peaches, apricots, quinces, etc.

Triploid – plants having three pairs of chromosomes, creating an odd number, and resulting in pollen that is neither self-fertile nor any good for fertilizing other fruit; when growing a triploid apple, such as *Bramley's Seedling*, pollen from a second apple tree is required to pollinate the *Bramley*, while a third tree is required to pollinate the second apple; family trees are a way of overcoming this problem when there is no space for three trees.

Upward-pointing bud – bud that is generally pointing up, away from the ground.

Variety – botanically, this refers to different plants of the same species that have occurred naturally, through evolution or as a result of nature producing a new 'sport' or chance seedling of an existing plant; for example, the *Bramley* is a variety of apple that was discovered after a chance seeding in a garden in Southwell, Nottinghamshire in 1809; in general gardening the term tends to be used interchangeably with cultivar.

Vine eye – a strong metal fixing used for training fruit; vine eyes screw into a wall or fence to support horizontal wires and hold the wires out from the surface by 7.5–10cm (3–4in), depending on size.

RESOURCES

There are many organizations that are of interest to anyone growing fruit, and fruit collections, large and small, can be found in most regions. Community orchards are springing up all over the place, as interest in growing fruit increases. Some plant nurseries run training courses in pruning, grafting and other ways of propagation. Most good garden centres will be able to give advice to customers buying fruit trees.

The following will be of particular interest to anyone wanting to learn more about growing fruit.

Common Ground

This organization has been at the forefront of reviving fruit growing in Great Britain, principally through promoting Apple Day events, which now take place in most counties throughout the country. In addition, Common Ground promotes fruit growing by offering ideas, information and inspiration through publications and projects such as Field Days, Parish Maps, Flora Britannica, Apple Day, Community Orchards, Tree Dressing Day, Confluence and the campaign for Local Distinctiveness.
www.commonground.org.uk

East of England Apples and Orchards Project

The East of England Apples and Orchards Project (EEAOP) is a registered charity working to guarantee a future for local orchard fruits and orchards. There are around 250 local varieties of apple, pear, plum and cherry that come from the seven counties of its core region – Bedfordshire, Cambridgeshire, Essex, Hertfordshire, Lincolnshire, Norfolk and Suffolk. EEAOP provides advice and has made available a selection of fruit tree varieties that originated in the East of England.
www.applesandorchards.org.uk

Garden Organic

Garden Organic, the UK's leading organic growing charity, has been at the forefront of the organic horticulture movement for fifty years and is dedicated to researching and promoting organic gardening, farming and food. It has collections of fruit growing under strictly organic conditions at its Ryton Gardens near Coventry, and in the kitchen garden at Audley End House in Essex.
www.gardenorganic.org.uk

Marcher Apple Network

The Marcher Apple Network (MAN) is dedicated to reviving the old apple and pear varieties in the Southern Marches, which covers the area of Herefordshire and the lower Wales–England border region, a traditional cider-producing area.
www.marcherapple.net

National Fruit Collection

The National Fruit Collection in Kent includes over 3,500 named apple, pear, plum, cherry, bush fruit, vine and cob-nut cultivars. The collection is owned

by the Department for the Environment, Food and Rural Affairs (Defra) and is part of an international programme to protect plant genetic resources for the future. The home of the National Fruit Collection is Brogdale Farm, Faversham, Kent.
www.nationalfruitcollection.org.uk
www.brogdalecollections.co.uk

Northern Fruit Group

The Northern Fruit Group aims to promote knowledge of fruit growing of all types, particularly those varieties suitable for growing in the north of England. It organizes displays, exhibitions, shows and meetings that are open to the public. It has set up registers of old fruit varieties and orchards in the north and advises on orchard establishment and maintenance.
www.northernfruitgroup.com

Plant Heritage

Plant Heritage is the world's leading garden plant conservation charity and runs the National Collection Scheme. Formerly known as the National Council for the Conservation of Plants & Gardens (NCCPG), Plant Heritage brings together the talents of botanists, horticulturalists and conservationists and the dedication of keen amateur and professional gardeners.
www.nccpg.com

Royal Horticultural Society (RHS)

The RHS Garden at Wisley in Surrey has an outstanding collection of fruit, including apples, pears, plums, quince, peaches and apricots, plus bush fruit, cane fruit, soft fruit and a vineyard. Fruit is grown in a range of different situations, from orchard scale to model fruit gardens that pack a lot of fruit into a relatively small space. There are examples of fruit that is trained in all the classic forms, and a range of fruit is displayed growing in containers. Other RHS gardens have some fruit, principally RHS Garden Rosemoor in Devon, which is growing varieties that are particularly suited to the conditions of southwest England.
www.rhs.org.uk/Gardens/Wisley
www.rhs.org.uk/Gardens/Rosemoor

RHS Fruit Group

Members of the RHS can join the RHS Fruit Group, a special interest group within the RHS which has a particular focus on all aspects of fruit and fruit growing. The RHS Fruit Group meets regularly at Wisley for talks, practical demonstrations and fruit tastings. There is a panel of experts on hand at meetings to answer questions on fruit growing, and each year the Group arranges a number of visits to fruit collections, commercial growers and gardens. The RHS Fruit Group also has active branches in the Southwest and the Midlands, and has very close links with the Northern Fruit Group.
Email: fruitgroupmembership@rhs.org.uk

Sources of Fruit Trees and Bushes

The fruit varieties mentioned in this book should be available from specialist fruit nurseries and good garden centres. Always try to buy good-quality plants that are certified as healthy. If you start off with a healthy plant, there is no reason why you should not be successful at growing fruit; if you start with a weak, unhealthy plant, you will always struggle, and your chances of growing good-quality fruit will be much reduced.

INDEX